The Complete
GOLFER'S
HANDBOOK

THE LYONS PRESS

The Complete
GOLFER'S
H A N D B O O K

Designer: Daniël Jansen van Vuuren
Publishing Manager and Editor: Mariëlle Renssen
Illustrators: James Berrangé, Daniël Jansen van Vuuren
Picture Research: Chris Whales, Duncan Cruickshank

Printed and bound in Singapore by Tien Wah Press (Pte) Ltd

THE AUTHORS WOULD LIKE TO THANK THE FOLLOWING PEOPLE WHOSE INPUT HAS CONTRIBUTED GREATLY TO PUTTING THIS BOOK TOGETHER: RONEL NEL OF THE GARY PLAYER GROUP FOR HER ONGOING INVALUABLE ASSISTANCE; DENNIS BRUYNS OF *COMPLEAT GOLFER* FOR HIS KNOWLEDGE OF GOLF'S HISTORY AND HIS ASSISTANCE IN CHOOSING THE 'MEMORABLE MOMENTS'; BERNARD MOSTERT FOR CONTRIBUTIONS, PARTICULARLY TO THE GOLF EQUIPMENT CHAPTER; ARNÉ CEDERVAL, WHOSE FINE SWING AND ACCEPTABLE FORM MADE THE OUTDOOR PHOTO SHOOTS AN EASY TASK; ANDREW LANNING, PETER MILNE AND JOHN CUMMOCK OF TOUCHLINE PHOTO, FOR THEIR UNTIRING HELP IN SOURCING THE BEST ACTION SHOTS WORLDWIDE; PHOTOGRAPHERS KELLY WALSH AND HETTIE ZANTMAN WHOSE PROFESSIONALISM AND PATIENCE MADE THEM A PLEASURE TO WORK WITH; MARK HARTNESS OF NEVADA BOB'S, CAPE TOWN, FOR THE GENEROUS LOAN OF EQUIP-MENT FOR THE PHOTO SHOOTS; AND TO EDITOR MARIËLLE RENSSEN AND DESIGNER DANIËL JANSEN VAN VUUREN, WHOSE KNOWLEDGE OF THE INTRICACIES AND BIZARRE QUIRKS OF THE GRAND OLD GAME OF GOLF NOW SURPASSES EVEN THEIR WILDEST IMAGINATION. WE LOOK FORWARD TO OUR FIRST GAME OF GOLF TOGETHER!

FOREWORD

Golf is not an easy game. It requires patience, concentration, and above all, hard work. Whether you are a beginner or a seasoned professional, you can never stop learning new things in this game, and you should never believe you know enough. One needs to watch other players, talk to them, and read as much as one can. Armed with knowledge, there is sure to be improvement, even if it is only curing a bad slice, adding a couple of yards to one's drives, or getting one's chips that little bit closer each time.

It is a great honour to be requested to write the foreword to a book by the great Gary Player. I have admired him ever since picking up a golf club for the first time as a young boy. Gary is well-known for his hard work, both on his game and his levels of fitness. He is forever looking to improve, despite the heights he has reached in his remarkable career. If only a small amount of this rubs off on the reader after studying this book, it has been time well spent.

Gary's determination and will to succeed for so long on golf courses around the world has been a wonderful inspiration to me. He has been a fine ambassador for our country as well as for the game of golf. A shining example of the ultimate sportsman, may he continue to weave his magic in international tournaments.

As a proud South African myself, playing golf tournaments across the world, it is always an honour to be compared with Gary Player. Considering our difference in size, however, I will only be happy with these comparisons once I've caught up in the number of Major victories! Now, there's something to aim for!

Ernie Els

CONTENTS

INTRODUCTION

The game of golf has evolved over the years into not only a multibillion-dollar industry, but also a sport accessible to many more people than ever before. Despite its attractiveness to large corporate sponsorship and the associated commercialism and hype, golf has been able to retain the traditions and spirit that make it unique.

It is the only ball sport where the action on the ball is dependent on one thing – the human being in control of the club that hits the ball. Unlike a game such as tennis, where a player has to react to a moving object hit by an opponent, a golfer has, comparatively speaking, all the time in the world to decide how to launch the ball in the direction of the hole. It is perhaps for this reason that golf is both the most satisfying – and the most frustrating – game known to man. As any golfer will know, once the 'bug' bites, it is very difficult to consign the clubs to the scrapheap and walk away from the game. Golf becomes an addiction – perhaps a healthier one than others – but difficult to give up, nonetheless.

Perhaps that is the reason for man's eternal search for the perfect swing, and all the books, periodicals and videos available that try to teach the 'ultimate way'. This book intends to give an overall understanding of the game as it is played today. Aimed at the novice, but also keeping the seasoned golfer in mind, there is advice for coping with every aspect of this often confusing game, ranging from explanations for various aspects of etiquette to advice on how best to play the bunker shot.

One of the world's greatest golfers, Gary Player, has contributed to this book with numerous pieces of advice learnt from nearly 50 years of travelling many thousands of air miles around our planet, playing in hundreds of tournaments – and winning a large number of them.

"GOLF IS A GAME IN WHICH A BALL – ONE AND A HALF INCHES IN DIAMETER – IS PLACED ON A BALL – 8000 MILES IN DIAMETER. THE OBJECT BEING TO HIT THE SMALL BALL BUT NOT THE LARGER."

— JOHN CUNNINGHAM

Tiger Woods rocketed to World Number One within months of his debut in professional golf, broadening the game's appeal across the world.

THE ORIGINS OF THE GAME

Man has always been attracted to pastimes involving hitting, throwing or kicking ball-like objects, although the actual origin of most ball games is lost in the mists of time. Golf is no exception and, while there are many theories surrounding the beginnings of the game, it is known that several different stick-and-ball games were played in medieval Europe.

One such game was *palle-maille*, played in the streets of France and Italy using a mallet-headed club to hit a small wooden ball towards a target which was either on the ground or elevated. The popularity of the game spread to Britain and the first *palle-maille* court was built in central London in the 17th century on a site known today as Pall Mall. A cross-country version of this game – *jeu de mail* – was also popular and courses were found in many parts of France; in fact, the game was still played in Montpellier in the 1930s.

Another medieval game was *chole*, played by Belgians on open pieces of land. A beech-wood ball was struck with a spoon-shaped metal club, the aim being to reach a distant target in as few strokes as possible. In neighbouring Holland the Dutch version, *colf*, was played mainly in the cities and often on ice, but the flying wooden balls proved difficult to control – and hazardous to passers-by – so a softer ball was made from leather, stuffed with feathers or cow hair. *Colf* was eventuazally replaced by *kolf*, an indoor version of the game.

In Scotland, the first written references to the game were recorded in the 15th century, when the

Above *Captain William Innes and caddy, in 1787, England.*

THE FIRST LADY GOLFER

The first recorded lady golfer, in 1563, was Mary, Queen of Scots (below), who played at St Andrews and in Edinburgh. Among her many misdemeanours, listed by the Earl of Moray in the 'Articles' he put before the Westminster Commissioners prior to her execution, was that she played golf only a few days after the murder of her husband, Lord Darnley.

For the hours he has spent playing golf, he has spent countless more practising. One of his most famous quotes, when told how lucky he always seemed to be, was: 'The harder I practise, the luckier I get!' Gary Player is also living proof of the importance of a strong mind when playing golf. If you are positive within yourself about your game, that is certainly half the battle won.

Dutch artist Hendrick Averkamp's painting of colf *being played on a frozen river.*

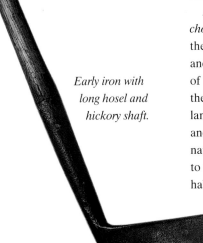

Early iron with long hosel and hickory shaft.

Right *One of the first 'gutta-percha' golf balls developed in the mid-19th century.*

parliament on several occasions banned golf – and other unmartial sports – as they were interfering with the practice of archery. In 1491 it was proclaimed that 'in na place of the realme there be usit Fute-ball, Golfe or uther sik unprofitabill sportis'. However, by the 16th century even the king himself was spending money on golf, and by the end of the century, golf in Scotland had evolved into a game resembling the one we play today.

Although several town games similar to *kolf* and *chole* were still being played in Scotland at this time, these became less popular as towns became busier and more organized, and this saw the increased use of 'links' land. Links refers to barren land between the windswept coastline and the agriculturally useful land further in; coastal sand was blown into dunes and covered by grass, resulting in terrain with severe natural undulations and sandy soil that was exposed to the mercy of the elements. These areas were not habitable or arable and they were generally used for grazing. Sheep would huddle together on the leeward side of bumps and ridges, rubbing themselves into the sandy soil to escape the wind – the resulting sandy hollows formed natural bunkers. Links land had few trees but extensive grassy areas kept short by grazing animals, making it ideal terrain for golf and, because of the sandy soil, the drainage was excellent and

play was often not suspended in even the heaviest of downpours. Golfers played on the land as they found it, using convenient features to shape the course – a hole would be placed at some distance from the previous one and a flattish piece of land would be made into a green. Only with the introduction of inland courses were man-made features incorporated and the advent of earth-moving machines created the banks, hollows and lakes found on modern courses.

By 1786 the game had spread to the USA – there were reports of Scottish officers playing in New York and a club had been formed in South Carolina – but it took over 100 years for the game to really take root in the USA. The first proper club in North America was formed in 1873 in Montreal, Canada, and it was soon given the 'Royal' prefix by the Queen. The British imperial, social and commercial expansions of the 19th century saw the start of a worldwide golf explosion. The game spread to the East – in India the Calcutta Golf Club was formed in 1829 and the Bombay Golf Club in 1842 – and in the Southern Hemisphere the first golf course, Dunedin Golf Club in Otago, New Zealand, was formed in 1871. South Africa followed in 1885 with Cape Town's Royal Cape Golf Club and Australia in 1891 with the formation of Royal Adelaide Golf Club.

The popularity of the game in the UK increased rapidly with the introduction of two competitons: the first 'Open' Championship (which developed into the British Open) was played in 1860 and the first Amateur Championship 25 years later. The British Open (held every year in July) is the oldest of the four 'modern' Major championships – the original Majors were the British and US Opens and the British and US Amateur Championships. The other three Majors today are the US Open (first held in 1895 and played every year in June), the US PGA Championship (introduced in 1916 and played in August) and the US Masters, the youngest of the Majors, begun in 1934 and played in April, and the only one held at the same course each year – Augusta National in Atlanta, Georgia. With the popularity of the game increasing throughout the 20th century, these four tournaments have captured the imagination of the golfing public and today form the highlights of an increasingly busy worldwide professional golfing calendar.

The home of golf – St Andrews, Scotland – in 1690.

In the past 100 or so years, the phenomenal rise of the game happened predominantly in four growth periods: the pioneer days of the 1890s when the number of clubs mushroomed from a handful to several hundred; the period following World War I which was inspired by US stars such as Bobby Jones, Walter Hagen and Gene Sarazen; the period following World War II when Americans such as Byron Nelson, Ben Hogan and Sam Snead again led the way; and the modern worldwide golf boom that has seen the sport become a billion-dollar industry.

HOME OF GOLF

St Andrews' epithet 'home of golf' (though not strictly correct – it is not the oldest club and the game didn't originate in Scotland) has been earned through the club's initiative in 1764 to reduce a full round of golf from 22 to 18 holes on its Old Course, and its role, in 1897, in formulating the Rules of Golf (thereafter becoming the major governing authority, in consultation with other governing bodies around the world).

THE MORRISES

Tom Morris Snr and Young Tom Morris were members of the most famous golfing family in the game. The elder Tom Morris grew up at the home of golf, St Andrews in Scotland, where at the age of 18 he was apprenticed to Allan Robertson to make feathery golf balls (*see* page 48). The two were also golf partners, forming an unbeaten partnership in the challenge matches of the time, but fell into disagreement over the introduction of the new gutty balls (*see* page 49), which Robertson opposed. Morris moved to Prestwick Golf Club on the west coast of Scotland where he became greenkeeper in 1851. It was here that Morris played a crucial role in setting up the first Open Championship – the forerunner of what was to become the world's most prestigious golf tournament, commonly known as the British Open. Morris started the first event as the favourite but in the end finished as runner-up to Willie Park Snr. Morris went on to win four Open Championships,

the last in 1867 at the age of 46. He was also runner-up on three occasions and finished fifth in 1881 when he was 60. He went on competing in the event until he was 75.

In 1865 he moved back to St Andrews where he was greenkeeper until 1904. He died four years later at the age of 87.

Tom Morris became known as Old Tom when his youngest son began to show exceptional golfing talent. Tom Morris Jnr, or Young Tom Morris, eventually eclipsed his father's successes in a short but spectacular career that established him as one of the greatest players the game has ever seen. Young Tom made his second appearance in the Open in 1867, finishing fourth, and the following year he returned to win the event, also recording the first hole-in-one in the tournament's history. He won again in 1869 and in 1870, a year in which his storming 149, a championship record that included a course record 47, gave him a 12-stroke victory. The teenager's three consecutive victories earned Young Tom outright possession of the Championship Belt. The event was suspended the following year pending the creation of a new trophy, the coveted Claret Jug still presented to winners today, and in 1872 Young Tom returned to win his fourth consecutive Open title. Sadly Tom died at the age of 24 – many believed from a broken heart – a few months after his beloved wife had died in childbirth.

A GOLFING TIMELINE

1360-1958

- **1360**
The first documentary reference to golf, in the Netherlands.
- **1457**
The first reference to golf in Scotland (football and golf are forbidden by parliament because they are interfering with military training), indicating that the Dutch possibly introduced the game to the Scots.
- **1502**
The first recorded golfer, James IV, buys clubs and balls.
- **1744**
The world's oldest golf club, the Honourable Company of Edinburgh Golfers, is formed and sets up the Silver Club competition.
- **1764**
The norm for a full round of golf becomes established when St Andrews in Scotland (1) reduces its Old Course from 22 holes to 18.
- **1786**
The first reference to golf in the United States of America when a club is formed at Charleston.
- **1829**
Royal Calcutta Golf Club in India becomes the first proper golf club formed outside the British Isles.
- **1834**
The Royal and Ancient title is conferred on St Andrews.

- **1848**
The gutta-percha ball is introduced.
- **1856**
The first golf club is established in continental Europe, at Pau, France.
- **1860**
The first Open Championship is staged at Prestwick Golf Club in Scotland, and is won by Scotsman Willie Park.
- **1861**
Old Tom Morris wins the second Open Championship. Together with his son, Young Tom, the Morrises win the event eight times between 1861 and 1872.
- **1864**
The Royal North Devon in Westward Ho! (2) is formed; it is today the oldest golf club in England still using its original course.
- **1870**
Young Tom Morris records a hat trick of Open Championship victories and retains the Championship Belt trophy (replaced in 1872 with the Claret Jug).
- **1885**
The first national amateur tournament, the British Amateur Championship, is held at Hoylake.
- **1885**
The first golf club in Africa, Royal Cape (3), is established in Cape Town, South Africa.

- **1891**
Royal Melbourne becomes the first golf course to open in Australia.
- **1892**
The Indian Amateur Championship is established – the world's oldest national tournament apart from the British Open and British Amateur.
- **1893**
The Royal and Ancient Golf Club of St Andrews (the R&A) declares that a 4.25in hole is mandatory for all golf courses.
Also The Ladies' Golf Union is founded in the UK.
- **1894**
The United States Golf Association (USGA) is formed.
- **1894**
J H Taylor (4) wins the British Open. Britons Taylor, James Braid and Harry Vardon, known as the Triumvirate, dominate the event by winning 16 Open Championships from 1894 to 1914.
- **1895**
The first US Open Championship is held at Newport, Rhode Island, and is won by Scotsman Willie Dunn.
Also The first US Amateur Championship is staged.
- **1897**
The R&A assumes responsibility for formulating the Rules of Golf.

- **1898**
Coburn Haskell of the UK patents the 'Haskell' golf ball.
- **1901**
The first golf course is opened in Japan, near Kobe.
- **1902**
'Rib-faced' clubs are introduced in an attempt to gain control over the Haskell ball.
- **1911**
Johnny McDermott becomes the first American-born winner of the US Open.
- **1914**
Harry Vardon wins a record sixth British Open and American Walter Hagen wins his first US Open.
- **1916**
The PGA of America is founded. The first US PGA Championship is held at Siwanoy, New York, and is won by 'Long' Jim Barnes. The second event is only held in 1919 after the end of World War I.
- **1919**
The R&A are appointed 'supreme ruling authority for the management and control of the game' and take over management of major British championships.
- **1921**
The R&A and USGA rule that a golf ball may not be more than 1.62oz in weight and 1.62in in diameter.

- **1922**
Aged only 20, tiny Gene Sarazen (**5**) wins two Majors, the US Open and US PGA. (In 1935 he wins the US Masters, completing his Grand Slam.)
- **1924**
Joyce Wethered of the UK wins her fifth consecutive English Ladies' Amateur.
- **1927**
The first Ryder Cup (**6**) is held in Worcester, Massachusetts, USA, and is won by the US team captained by Walter Hagen, who also wins his fourth consecutive – fifth in total – US PGA title.
- **1929**
The R&A, following the lead set by the USGA in 1926, legalizes steel shafts.
- **1930**
Bobby Jones completes the first ever Grand Slam – winning the US Open, US Amateur, British Open and British Amateur in the same year.
- **1932**
The USA beats the UK in the first Curtis Cup match.
- **1934**
The first US Masters Tournament is held at Augusta, Georgia (**7**) , the golf course created by the legendary Bobby Jones. It is won by American Horton Smith.

- **1945**
Byron Nelson of the USA wins 19 tournaments in 31 starts, including 11 consecutive victories.
- **1946**
American Ben Hogan wins his first Major, the US PGA Championship. Fellow US golfer Sam Snead wins his only British Open, but expresses disgust with the course, his caddie, the accommodation and the food.
- **1948**
US Olympic star Babe Zaharias, probably the greatest female athlete of all time, wins the first of her three US Women's Open titles.
- **1951**
The R&A and USGA hold a rules conference; the 'stymie' is abolished.
- **1953**
Ben Hogan becomes the first – and only – golfer to win three modern Majors in a year (US Masters, US Open and British Open).
- **1957**
The Britain and Ireland Ryder Cup team, captained by Dai Rees, records the first win over the USA in 34 years.
- **1958**
Arnold Palmer (**8**) of the USA wins his first Major, the US Masters. He wins it four times, plus two British Opens and a US Open.

A GOLFING TIMELINE

9

10

11

1959 ONWARDS

- **1959**
Gary Player wins his first Major, the British Open (**9**). In 1965 he becomes only the fourth player to win all four Majors, and in 1978, at 42, he wins his ninth Major, the US Masters.
Also Mickey Wright becomes the first woman to win back-to-back US Women's Open titles.

- **1962**
US golfer Jack Nicklaus, aged 22, beats Arnold Palmer in a play-off to win the US Open (first of 18 Major victories).

- **1965**
Australian Peter Thomson wins his fifth British Open.

- **1968**
'Croquet' style putting is banned.

- **1971**
Lee Trevino wins the US, Canadian and British Opens over a period of three weeks.

- **1972**
The European Tour is launched.

- **1974**
Gary Player wins the British Open, playing with the obligatory 1.68in ball.

- **1978**
American Nancy Lopez wins five consecutive events in the USA, tripling the gate at US LPGA events.

- **1979**
Seve Ballesteros (**10**) becomes the first Spaniard, and the first continental European since 1907, to win the British Open. In 1980 Ballesteros becomes the first European – and at 23 the youngest player – ever to win the US Masters.

- **1980**
The US Senior Tour is launched with just two tournaments – it grows to over 40 events by the mid-1990s.

- **1983**
American Tom Watson (**11**) joins Australian Peter Thomson as a five-time modern British Open champion.

- **1986**
Jack Nicklaus (**12**) becomes the oldest US Masters winner at age 46.

- **1986**
Greg Norman wins the first of his two British Opens (**13**). The blond Australian goes on to dominate the game for nearly a decade.

- **1987**
Nick Faldo of the UK wins his first Major, the British Open, after rebuilding his swing under the guidance of David Leadbetter. Faldo goes on to win six Majors.

- **1990**
Nick Faldo wins his second consecutive US Masters (**14**) as well as the British Open at St Andrews.
Also Betsy King of the USA wins her second consecutive US Women's Open title.

- **1993**
German Bernhard Langer, one of Europe's most consistent performers, wins his second US Masters title.

- **1994**
British golfer Laura Davies (**15**) tops the US money list; she becomes the first golfer (male or female) to win events on five different tours.

- **1996**
Australia's Greg Norman lets slip a six-shot lead in the final round of the US Masters to hand victory to Nick Faldo.

12

13

14

15

16

- **1997**

  American Tiger Woods **(16)** wins the
  US Masters in his first year as a professional, setting new world records.

- **1998**

  Scotland's Colin Montgomerie heads
  the European Tour Order of Merit for
  a sixth consecutive year.

  Also Mark O'Meara **(17)** wins two
  Majors – the US Masters and British
  Open – as well the World Matchplay.

  Also South Korean wondergirl Se Ri
  Pak wins two US LPGA Majors in her
  début year and is named Rookie of the
  Year, LPGA Player of the Year and
  AP Female Athlete of the Year.

- **1999**

  David Duval stages the most dramatic
  comeback in US PGA Tour history
  when he shoots a 13-under-par final
  round of 59 to win the Bob Hope
  Chrysler Classic, becoming only the
  third person in the Tour's history to
  break 60.

17

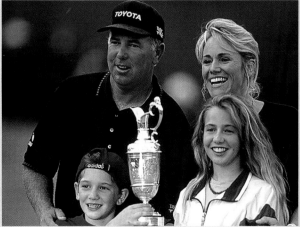

Previous pages *The gallery*
at the £1250 News of the
World tournament at Oxhey,
Hertfordshire, in 1936.

THE GAME TODAY

Golf as we know it today has evolved considerably from the time of the Honourable Company of Edinburgh Golfers. Courses are being designed

remained as it was 20 years ago, which suggests that golf remains as difficult a game as it always was. Golf as we know it today is played by perhaps four distinct groups of people – the touring and club professionals, the competitive amateurs, the amateur 'club' golfers and the beginners or occasional 'hackers'.

Professional golf has become an extremely lucrative career for those who are able to win tournaments and make cuts on the major tours, but at the same time it is an extremely harsh way of trying to earn a living for the vast majority of those who choose to join the paid ranks. There are a myriad professional golf tours worldwide, ranging from the so-called 'mini-tours' to the European Tour and the US PGA Tour. Top professionals easily earn in excess of a million dollars a year on the major tours in prize money alone, before taking into account the sponsorship and endorsement deals that bring in countless more millions every year.

Amateur golf still plays a major role, with numerous prestigious titles on offer such as the British and the US Amateur Championships. Amateur team competitions are still played, with golfers representing their countries and playing for

Tiger Woods turned professional in 1996 after winning an unprecedented three consecutive US Amateur titles. He immediately signed a US$40 million endorsement deal with Nike.

Young Justin Rose tied fourth
in the 1998 British Open.

and built all over the world including such places as mainland China, which is experiencing a boom in golf development.

Television, too, has played its role in beaming images of tournament golf to millions of homes throughout the world.

As technology in our daily lives has improved, so too has the design and marketing of golf equipment. Millions of dollars are spent annually on research and development of clubs that claim to hit the ball straighter and more consistently, and balls that fly further with better and more consistent spin. Countless more millions of dollars are poured into the marketing of these wonder products, with ever increasing numbers looking for a slice of this very lucrative, yet competitive market.

Interestingly, with all the advancements in technology, the average handicap of golfers has

nothing more than the honour and glory of winning. However, the world's top amateurs tend to be youngsters using these tournaments as stepping stones to the paid ranks. There is usually a frenzy as sponsors line up to make lucrative offers to the youngsters, hoping for another Tiger Woods. A good example is the UK's Justin Rose, who at the tender age of 17 years, put up a sparkling performance in the 1998 British Open. Sponsors queued up to sign endorsement deals with him, and he turned professional the following day. For every superstar, however, there are possibly a thousand talented amateurs who disappear into obscurity.

Although golf has spread around the world and gained in popularity, it remains an expensive pastime, requiring large investments of both time and money by the player who gets bitten by the proverbial 'bug'.

GARY PLAYER

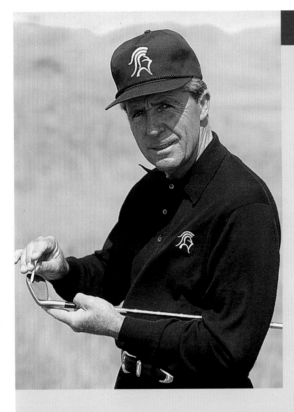

Gary Player is South Africa's greatest golfer. The world's most travelled athlete, he has amassed over nine million air miles crossing the globe, and he has won over 150 tournaments worldwide. He won the British Open in three different decades (in 1959, 1968 and 1974), he's one of four men to win all four Majors and he has won nine in total – three US Masters, three British Opens, two PGA Championships and one US Open. In 1988 he completed the Senior Grand Slam, becoming the only man ever to win both the Regular and Senior Grand Slams.

Born on 1 November 1935 in Johannesburg, Player achieved well in schoolboy sports, despite his small stature (he is 5ft 7in, or 1.68m, tall) and shortly before his 15th birthday he reluctantly accepted his father's invitation to join him for a game of golf at the Virginia Park course where Harry Player was a low handicapper. Gary parred the first three holes he played and was hooked.

Within 16 months he had developed into a scratch player and in 1953, after completing his schooling, he went to work as an assistant to golf pro Jock Verwey at Virginia Park. He lived with Verwey (whose daughter Vivienne immediately caught Player's eye). Player decided that the way to fulfil his ambition of becoming one of the greatest golfers in the world was by learning from the best and playing in other parts of the world. On his first trip outside South Africa that year, his lone victory came in Egypt where he won a matchplay tournament. The next year he won twice at home (including his first SA Open), once in Britain and once in Australia. With ample prize money in hand he phoned Vivienne Verwey and told her to get herself a wedding dress. They were married shortly thereafter.

Player's father was responsible for bringing about his first trip to the USA. Harry wrote to Clifford Roberts, then chairman of the US Masters tournament, urging him to invite his son to play in 1957. Roberts did and Player competed in his first event at Augusta. Over 40 years later, Player has missed only one US Masters, and in 1998 he became the oldest golfer ever to make the cut in the Masters. Player became a regular and consistent winner on the US PGA Tour, where he gained attention for his forceful tee shots – which threw him off balance after the ball was in the air.

Player favoured black attire which resulted in him being branded the 'Black Knight'. He developed a fitness and exercise regime long before it was fashionable, and his work ethic is illustrated by the now-famous words: 'The more I practise, the luckier I get.'

Over the years he diversified his interests, forming the Gary Player Group which expanded into various other fields, including golf course design and golf equipment manufacture. The Players have six children and 10 grandchildren, a home at Blair Atholl on the outskirts of Johannesburg and a stud farm in Colesberg, South Africa, and a US base in Palm Beach, Florida.

Despite his height, Player's determination and tenacity have made him one of the biggest names in world golf.

CHAPTER TWO

ETIQUETTE
AND RULES

ETIQUETTE

The *Oxford English Dictionary*'s definition of etiquette is, among others: 'Conventional rules of personal behaviour in polite society'. The game of golf is probably the only sport where the unwritten rules of etiquette are as important – in many cases more so – as the official rules themselves. Indeed, many of the finer points of etiquette are included as part of the official Rules of the Game.

Previous pages *The Royal & Ancient Golf Club of St Andrews, Scotland.*

Golf etiquette is something every golfer, whether a complete novice or a seasoned professional, should have a thorough working knowledge of and should always be looking to improve.

Most of the traditions of golf have managed to survive the changing times since the Honourable Company of Edinburgh Golfers first started putting quill to paper to record the rules of their game. Today, golf still has the reputation for being the game where sportsmanship and honour survive, despite the worldwide boom in popularity during the latter half of the 20th century. However, it is clear that golf is fast losing its exclusivity and becoming the game of the masses as a result of the influx of sponsorship money and live televised events beamed by satellite around the world.

"THE NICE THING ABOUT THESE GOLF BOOKS IS THAT THEY USUALLY CANCEL EACH OTHER OUT. ONE BOOK TELLS YOU TO KEEP YOUR EYE ON THE BALL; THE NEXT SAYS NOT TO BOTHER. PERSONALLY, IN THE CROWD I PLAY WITH, A BETTER IDEA IS TO KEEP YOUR EYE ON YOUR PARTNER."

— *JIM MURRAY*

So just what is golf etiquette, and why is it so important? Etiquette is simply about courtesy and consideration of fellow players, both on and off the golf course. (Bear in mind you're sharing a large area of open land with people, all of whom have the intent of launching a dangerous missile!) Etiquette makes for a safer and more enjoyable game for all.

The easiest way to describe the various etiquette 'rules' is to deal with them in a chronological order, starting with arranging a game, and working through to setting off for a round.

BEFORE THE GAME

Booking a tee-off time is usually essential; this can be done via the telephone, and is usually a good first contact with a club at which one is not a member. Various questions can be asked of the club secretary, manager or club professional at this time in

'Plus-fours' are so named as the overhang at the knee requires an extra four inches.

has been found to leave a change of clothes, or at least one's shoes.

Clothes are often a controversial aspect of the golfer's life and every club will have dress codes that have to be adhered to. If your choice of clothing is unacceptable to the club or course on which you are intending to play, you can be assured that you will not be permitted to play. To avoid such embarrassment, ensure that you check beforehand what the particular club regulations stipulate.

Clubs usually require a jacket and tie to be worn in certain areas of the clubhouse; again this should be verified before arrival to avoid being turned away.

LOCAL RULES

Of great importance before starting to play a round at any club is to make sure that the local rules have been noted. Often a club will introduce rules according to prevailing weather conditions, or physical conditions on the course itself, such as ground-under-repair or placing on the fairways. There may be permanent local rules as well, such as out-of-bounds areas that would not normally be considered out-of-bounds at other courses.

SETTING OFF

Having checked your equipment, any requirements such as balls and tees should be purchased at the Pro Shop. There is nothing that frustrates other golfers more than to have to hand out tees or balls during a round to an unprepared playing partner.

American Payne Stewart is one of the more colourful dressers on today's pro tours.

DRESS REGULATIONS

At almost every club around the world, strict dress codes apply. Standard regulations are:

• **For Men**: No T-shirts, vests or shorts without a belt.

• Some clubs still require long socks to be worn with shorts (although it seems this is being phased out around the world).

• No matter how expensive, jeans are still unacceptable.

• Shirts should have a collar.

• In certain areas of the clubhouse (e.g. the members' bar) men may be required to wear jacket and tie.

• **For Women**: The regulations tend to be restricted to length of shorts above the knee.

order to avoid any embarrassing situations at the club. For example, the cost of green fees can be confirmed, as can the requirements regarding spiked shoes, caddie carts, dress regulations, and the like.

Once the game has been arranged, punctual arrival at the course is essential. Lateness with respect to tee-off times is unacceptable, not only because it holds up your playing partners, but it also disrupts the rest of the field.

On arrival at the club and before setting off for the first tee, the first-time golfer should ensure that green fees are paid, that the visitors' book is signed – often a legal requirement if the club is licensed and bar facilities are going to be used – and that the locker room has been located and a suitable place

SPEED OF PLAY

Generally four to four and a half hours is more than enough time for a four-ball to complete 18 holes of golf. This is of course dependent on many different factors, such as the type of competition, the number of players in the field and the type of course being played. If you are a tortoise on the course, here are a number of suggestions to speed up play.

- Be ready to play your shot when it's your turn; while other players are playing their shots, make decisions about club choice, etc.
- Watch the flight of your ball carefully, and note how it lands if possible. If it's heading for the trees, take note of which tree, so that when you get nearer, you'll know the general area in which to search.
- Do not waste time on the green: read the line of your putt while others are putting and don't waste time with unnecessary practice putts while standing over the ball.
- Mark your card off the green; move swiftly from the green to the next tee.
- Walk quickly between shots.

Warm-up Once this has all been carried out, the golfer should now shift his focus of attention to the game itself, and depending on the seriousness of the round, commence his warm-up routine. This is best done away from the first tee as many clubs do not allow practice swings on the tee itself. Be considerate of other golfers around you when you practise swinging: ensure that there are no fellow golfers standing behind you as you start your warm-up routine. If you are playing in a serious competition, or if time allows, a visit to the practice ground is advisable for your warm-up. Here, you can actually hit balls and be fully prepared to play once your tee becomes available.

Play On the first tee, once you are ready to play, wait either for the starter to tell you that you may begin, or in the absence of a starter, wait until the group ahead is well out of range of the best possible tee shot of the first player on the tee. Let the players in front play their second shots and then only walk forward to begin your round. As with most things on the golf course, let common sense prevail when making such decisions. Remember, these people are likely to be ahead of you for the next four hours or so – the last thing you want to do is have them irate on the first hole!

The best place to stand when awaiting your turn on the tee is adjacent to the player teeing off, and slightly behind. You have to be especially vigilant if you have a left-hander in your group. The general rule is to stay alert, so as to not distract your playing partner, and for your own safety.

Always watch the flight of your playing partners' ball, and mark it against an object on the hole so as to make finding it simpler. This will help to speed up the process of looking for a ball that has been lost.

Once everyone in your group has played their tee shots, set off for the fairway without delay. A day out on the course should be savoured, but not treated as a late afternoon stroll.

ORDER OF PLAY

The rules of golf state that the person furthest from the hole should play first. If you are generally shortest off the tee and therefore likely to have to play first off the fairway, try to plan your next shot as you approach your ball. By doing so you will save time when you reach the ball and have to select a club for your next shot. If you are not sure whether you are in fact furthest from the hole, you do not have to get out the measuring tape. As with most aspects of etiquette, let common sense prevail, and communicate with your playing partners. Once you have played your shot, carry out any course maintenance required and move quickly to a safe position from which to watch your partners' shots.

THE RULES OF GOLF

The Royal and Ancient Golf Club of St Andrews (or R&A as it is known), in St Andrews, Scotland, is one of the game's oldest golf clubs and certainly the most influential club in the world. Founded in 1754 by 22 'noblemen and gentlemen' as the Society of St Andrews Golfers, the R&A played a major role in the development of the game and, in 1897, at the suggestion of leading clubs in the UK, it became the governing authority on the Rules of Golf. The Rules are published by the R&A, in con-

The clubhouse of the R&A, St Andrews.

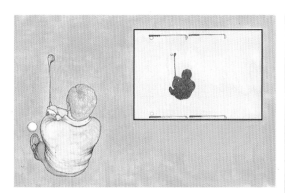

Teeing off: place ball between tee markers (although you may stand outside the markers), and not more than two club-lengths behind markers.

sultation with the United States Golf Association (USGA) and golfing bodies throughout the world, and translated into around 20 different languages. While the basic rules of golf seldom change, a volume of *Decisions on the Rules of Golf* is published each year, focusing on new and special situations not already covered in the Rules.

For the average or novice golfer, however, a knowledge of the fundamental rules of the game is sufficient – but essential. There are three important principles to remember when playing golf:
1. Play the course as you find it.
2. Play the ball as it lies.
3. If you can't do either, do what is fair.

Play the ball as it lies; it is illegal to flatten grass behind the ball to improve the lie.

GARY PLAYER'S INTERPRETATION OF THE BASIC RULES

- The honour of teeing off first belongs to the player with the lowest handicap on the first tee, and on subsequent holes to the best score on the previous hole.
- On the tee, the ball is placed either on the ground or on a tee peg in the area just behind the two markers, two club-lengths behind the markers at most.
- After the tee shot, the player who lands furthest from the hole is the one to play first.
- Should you lose your ball, you are allowed five minutes to find it. If the search is unsuccessful, play another ball from the tee (if the lost ball was played from here) or, if it was not your first shot, drop a ball from shoulder height as near as possible to the spot from which you hit the ball that was lost. A penalty shot is added to your score for the lost ball.
- Should you hit your ball out-of-bounds (marked with white stakes or as described in Local Rules), proceed as for a lost ball.
- Except for a ball in a water hazard, you can declare any ball unplayable. You have three alternatives to continue your game with an extra penalty stroke:

1. Play your next stroke from as near as possible to the spot where your original ball was played.
2. Drop a ball within two club-lengths of the spot where the ball lay, but not nearer to the hole.
3. Drop a ball behind the spot where the ball lay, keeping that spot directly between yourself and the hole. There is no limit as to how far behind that spot the ball may be dropped.

- Should you land in a water hazard marked with yellow stakes or yellow lines (indicating a pond, lake or stream), you may drop a ball as far back as you

COURSE MAINTENANCE

Keeping a course in top condition throughout the year has enormous cost implications. It is essential that every golfer does his bit to repair any damage that he may inflict on the course when hitting the ball.

- Divots: depending on Local Rules, fill the hole with sand from the sand bag you carry with you or replace the piece of turf.
- On the tee: replace or repair divots. Pick up broken or discarded pegs.
- Bunkers: although these are designed to be hazards, it is unfair for a golfer to have to play out of your footprints or unsmoothed sand. Use the rake provided and smooth the sand completely so as to remove any evidence of your having been there.
- On the green: make sure you have a pitch mark repairer, and use it to repair the indentation made by your ball when it lands on the green. Always try to repair more than just your own pitch mark on the green.
- Don't lean on your putter, or do anything that will damage the green with your shoes. Extra care should be taken when in close proximity to the hole. The rules do not allow the repair of spike marks on the green, so be extra careful if you are wearing spikes.
- Be careful how and where you place the flagstick when you remove it to putt. Preferably place it on the fringe of the green. If you are holding it, do not lean on it!

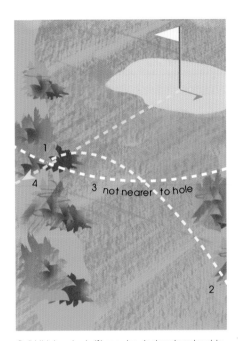

Ball hit into a bush (1) may be declared unplayable. For a one-stroke penalty, player may replay shot from original position (2), or drop within two club-lengths from ball's position (3) but not nearer hole, or drop behind ball's position (4).

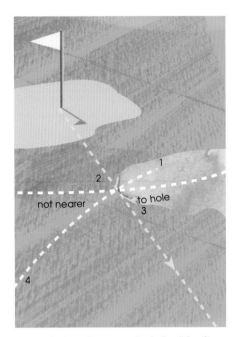

From water hazard, you may play ball as it lies (1), or drop within two club-lengths of where ball crossed edge of hazard (2) but not nearer hole, or drop on a line between hole and point of entry to water hazard (3), or replay shot from original position (4).

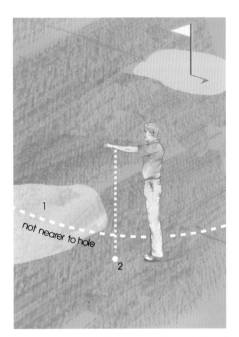

Ground-under-repair (1): you may pick up ball and drop it within one club-length of nearest point of relief (2). However, this may not be nearer the hole. There is no penalty.

KEY TO ILLUSTRATIONS ABOVE	
Yellow:	initial shot
White:	ball may not be moved
	closer to the hole
Blue:	possible line of play

Unplayable lie.

like while keeping the point where the ball entered the water between you and the hole.

- Should the ball be lost in a lateral water hazard (one which is roughly parallel to the line of the hole and is marked with red stakes), you may drop the ball within two club-lengths of the point level with where the lost ball entered, on either side of the hazard but not nearer the hole. The penalty for dropping out of a water hazard is one stroke.
- Should your ball lie on the green in another player's putting line, you are required to lift your ball after placing a ball marker or coin behind your ball.
- When putting on the green, the flag should always be removed from the hole as there is a two-stroke penalty for hitting the flag.

LOCAL RULES

One of the final Rules of Golf states: 'The Committee may make and publish Local Rules for abnormal conditions if they are consistent with the policy of the governing authority for the country concerned as set forth in Appendix 1 of these Rules.

HOW TO DROP A BALL

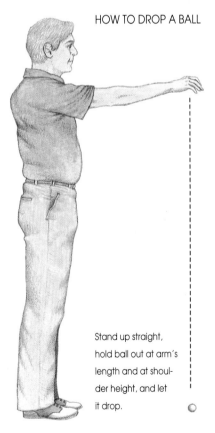

Stand up straight, hold ball out at arm's length and at shoulder height, and let it drop.

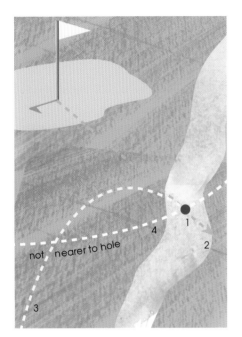

Ball in a lateral water hazard: play ball as it lies (1) or, for a one-stroke penalty, drop on a line behind hazard (2), or replay shot from original position (3), or play from within two club-lengths from point of entry (4) but not nearer hole.

A penalty imposed by a Rule of Golf shall not be waived by a Local Rule.' In other words, a golf club committee can decide to impose Local Rules which apply to its golf club only to cover special situations or circumstances that may arise due to peculiarities of that golf course. The Local Rules are usually printed on the scorecard provided at the club or may be posted on the notice board. Always be sure to read them before commencing your round.

Local Rules generally provide guidelines for dealing with:

1. Obstructions: unusual objects and constructions; stones in bunkers; roads and paths; fixed sprinkler heads; young trees that must be protected; and temporary obstructions such as grandstands, television equipment, etc.
2. Areas of the course requiring preservation such as turf nurseries, ground-under-repair, etc.
3. Unusual damage to the course or the accumulation of leaves or the like.

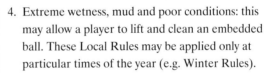

REMEMBER THE STYMIE?

Prior to 1952, a player was 'stymied' on the green if he was unable to putt directly towards the hole because his opponent's ball lay in the way. Unless the balls lay within 6in (15cm) of each other, the only solution was to try to loft the ball over the obstacle or to use the contours of the green to play around it. Traditionalists wanted to keep the stymie for two reasons – because it had been part of the game for so long (it had been in force since 1812, apart from one year in 1833 when the R&A abandoned the rule but reimposed it the following year) and because doing away with the stymie would allow lifting of the ball, which was contrary to the 'play it as it lies' school of thinking. At a 1952 rules conference between the R&A and the USGA, the stymie rule was voted out of the game of golf by 25 votes to 22.

4. Extreme wetness, mud and poor conditions: this may allow a player to lift and clean an embedded ball. These Local Rules may be applied only at particular times of the year (e.g. Winter Rules).
5. Environmentally sensitive areas on the course.
6. The status of sections of water hazards.
7. The definition of margins or boundaries of out-of-bounds, hazards, water hazards, lateral water hazards and ground-under-repair.
8. Providing special dropping zones for when a ball may need to be dropped.
9. Priority on the course and regulations governing etiquette.

The spirit and cameraderie of golf make it special.

Carry a towel and clean your ball regularly.

Mark your ball for easy identification during play.

Use a pitch mark repairer to repair indentations made by your ball on the green.

CHAPTER THREE

PLAYING
THE COURSE

Previous pages *A golfer taking part in the 1992 US Masters tournament at Augusta National in Atlanta, Georgia, USA.*

Golf is a unique sport in that the arena in which it is played is not only vast, but that every golf course is a unique playing ground. What makes golf such an exciting game is that it is virtually impossible to repeat any one course. If that were possible, there would probably be many Augusta Nationals dotted across the planet. The look of a golf course is largely determined by the land on which it is built and is dependent on many factors. But every golf course has certain features in common and the standard elements that make up the average course are as follows:

THE TEE
This is the area from which the first shot is played for each hole. It is usually a raised piece of ground with a similar grass covering as that on the fairways. A pair of tee markers is positioned perpendicular to the fairway on either side of the tee (peg) from behind which the golfer tees up his ball to play his first shot. The ball may be teed anywhere between these markers as long as it is not in front of them and not more than two club-lengths behind (*see* page 29). The player is allowed to take his stance outside the markers, but the ball must be between them. The tee markers may not be moved.

When placing the ball on the teeing ground, a player may place it on a tee, alternatively he can

"I'M HITTING THE DRIVER SO GOOD, I GOTTA DIAL THE OPERATOR FOR LONG DISTANCE AFTER I HIT IT."

— *LEE TREVINO*

make a mound using his foot or a club. Should the ball fall from the peg or mound before the player makes a stroke at it, he may replace it and start again. If, however, it falls while the player is in the process of swinging at it, he is deemed to have played a stroke.

On most courses there are separate tees for 'championship play', men's club tees and ladies' tees, the major difference being the distance from the green – the championship tee is furthest away and the ladies' tee closest.

FAIRWAY
The fairway is the closely mown area between tee and green at each hole, and it is usually surrounded by very rough grass, trees or other hazards on either side. The fairway is obviously the area to which any

There are no limits laid down as to the size of bunkers on a golf course.

DIVOTS

These are pieces of turf hit out of the ground along with the ball, mostly by iron shots. Divots are frustrating to golfers if left unrepaired. Relief from a divot cannot be obtained without penalty unless Local Rules allow for placing on the fairway, in which case the ball can be moved back onto the fairway, but not nearer the hole. Many courses prefer that divots are repaired by filling them with sand and not just replacing the disturbed turf, as the sod tends to die rather than regrow.

DISTANCE MARKERS

Most courses have fairly accurate distance markers placed on or near the fairway to assist the player with club selection. These are commonly seen in the form of a solitary small tree on the side of the fairway, or as painted sprinkler heads, or even granite stones placed in the middle of the fairway (these can be treated as immovable obstructions if the ball comes to rest on them). Distance markers are most often placed some 165yd (150m) from the front or the middle of the green. It is wise to confirm which of the two options applies before setting out on the course for obvious reasons.

ROUGH

The rough is the area that all golfers try to avoid at all costs, but every golfer visits more often than he would prefer. There is usually 'semi-rough' on the edges of the fairway which is really fairway on which grass has been allowed to grow longer. Depending on the competition being played on the course, the severity of this area can be allowed to vary, thereby altering the difficulty of the course. The rough itself can be made up of any kind of terrain depending on the course's location. It can vary from totally

Ben Crenshaw takes a large divot out of the thick rough.

golfer would like to hit his tee-shot on a par four or par five. It is usually obvious where fairway ends and rough begins, but the condition of the course can make it somewhat confusing.

This is important to know, especially when there are Local Rules that allow for the placing of the ball on the fairway. Placing is not allowed in the rough, so a golfer will often find himself confirming with his playing partners whether his ball is indeed on the fairway or not. Golfers have been known to try to stretch the definition of 'fairway' when faced with a tricky lie!

The advantage of the fairway is that it is where the golfer will have the best lie from which to play his approach shot, allowing him to make the cleanest contact with the ball, thereby ensuring the best flight and result for his shot.

PAR CLARIFIED

Every golf course has a unique scorecard (available to all golfers) which gives the distance, par and difficulty rating for each hole on that course. Par is the number of strokes in which each player is expected to complete a particular hole.

Nick Faldo indicates his position to his caddy after a particularly wayward shot.

between club face and ball, the shot becomes a lot less predictable, and therefore more difficult. Therefore a bad shot played into the rough is usually further punished because the shot to get out of trouble is that much harder. This is incentive enough to play straight and keep to the fairway at all costs.

LOOSE IMPEDIMENTS

Loose impediments are found all over most golf courses, and consist of natural objects such as twigs, leaves, stones, worms, insects – in fact,

EXAMPLES OF 'LOOSE IMPEDIMENTS' FOUND ON THE COURSE

unmanaged natural terrain to long, uncut fairway grass. The disadvantage of landing in the rough is that there are usually other obstructions within that area, for example, trees, and also because the lies are likely to be far worse than on the fairway. As soon as the golfer is unable to ensure clean contact almost anything that is not actually growing out of the ground. Sand and loose soil are only loose impediments on the green and not elsewhere.

Loose impediments may be cleared from around the golfer's ball or stance; however this cannot be done when both the ball and the loose impediment are lying in the same hazard. If in the action of clearing the loose impediment the ball moves, the player incurs a penalty under the Rules.

Snow and natural ice can be defined, at the option of the player, as either water, or casual water, or loose impediments.

CASUAL WATER

Casual water is any temporary accumulation of water on the course which is visible before or after the player takes his stance and is not in an existing water

Seve Ballesteros retrieves his ball from casual water.

hazard. Relief from casual water may be obtained without penalty by dropping the ball to the nearest dry piece of ground. Relief from casual water in a bunker may also be obtained, but the ball must be dropped within the bunker.

GROUND-UNDER-REPAIR (GUR)

Ground-under-repair is any portion of the course marked by the Committee as such and includes material piled for removal and holes made by the greenkeeper. It is always marked, either by means of stakes or lines, or defined in Local Rules. If a player's ball comes to rest in GUR, relief may be obtained without penalty. Golfers must be aware that loose or abandoned cuttings or other material left on the course are not necessarily GUR and need to be defined as such.

OBSTRUCTIONS

In golf there are two types of obstructions: immovable and movable. The Rules of Golf define an obstruction as being: 'anything artificial, including the artificial surfaces and sides of roads and paths and manufactured ice except: a) objects defining out-of-bounds such as walls, fences, stakes or railings; b) any part of an artificial object which is out-of-bounds; and c) any construction declared by the Committee to be an integral part of the course'.

This last exception has caused the downfall of many professional golfers playing in a tournament when their ball has come to rest on or near an advertising board. They often do not study the tournament rules closely enough, and take relief when this is not permissible, thereby incurring penalties that can prove to be rather costly.

Relief can be obtained from obstructions without incurring any penalty as long as they are not in hazards or bunkers.

OUT-OF-BOUNDS

Out-of-bounds is simply ground on which play is prohibited. It is defined by stakes (usually white) or railings, and any part of the ball that is within its confines is out-of-bounds. However, a player may stand within the out-of-bounds in order to play a ball that has come to rest in-bounds. If a shot results in the ball going into the out-of-bounds area, the golfer should treat it as lost and play his next shot from where he last played as well as incurring a one-stroke penalty.

The Committee can often declare an adjoining fairway out-of-bounds in order to prohibit golfers from taking dangerous short-cuts to the green.

HAZARDS
Bunkers

Bunkers, or sand traps, probably cause most golfers more fear and heartache than they should, because they are fairly easily negotiated with the right technique. Bunkers occur both around the green as well as in and beside fairways. The depth varies according to their location and to the consistency and type of sand. Fairway bunkers will usually be shallower than their greenside counterparts, but there is no hard and fast rule on this. It depends largely on the whims of the golf course architect or the Club Committee

A golf course undergoing maintenance.

Previous pages *The par four 18th hole at the Portmarnock Golf Links Course in Dublin, Ireland; the course was designed by German golfer Bernhard Langer.*

of the time. Railway sleepers are not uncommon as edging for a bunker and are usually declared 'an integral part of the course'.

The Rules of Golf do not allow for the testing of the surface of a hazard, so a golfer may not 'ground' his club (come into contact with the earth) behind the ball while preparing to play out of the bunker. Also, loose impediments may not be moved away from the ball, adding to the player's difficulties.

Rakes used to smooth a bunker after a shot has been played are movable obstructions anywhere on the course and may be moved if interfering with the ball or the shot in the bunker. If the ball moves while removing the rake, it must be replaced and there is no penalty as long as the movement is only caused by moving the rake. It is sound etiquette not only to ensure that the rake is used to smooth the ground after playing a shot in the bunker, but also to place it as far out of the way as possible so as not to interfere with a following shot by another golfer. Footprints and other disturbed sand caused by thoughtless golfers who fail to smooth the bunker are considered irregularity of surface, from which relief without penalty is not available. Any golfer who has had to play from an oversize footprint in soft sand will not exactly be smiling when emerging from the bunker.

Water hazards

These can vary in size from the smallest stream to a stretch of ocean and are usually defined as either water hazards or lateral water hazards.

Lateral water hazards are water hazards, or parts of water hazards, that are deemed impossible or impractical to drop behind. They are specifically marked as such, usually by means of red stakes. For example, a stream running parallel to a fairway from tee to green would be a lateral water hazard and the following steps should be taken when dropping a ball from the hazard. Because there is nowhere to drop behind the hazard, the golfer must play either within two club-lengths from the point of entry into the hazard, or as far back along the line of flight of the ball as he wishes, right up to where he played his last shot. He could also drop a ball on the other side of the lateral hazard as long as it is equidistant from the hole. Often a demarcated dropping zone for a water hazard from which the player can play will be established by the Committee.

Of course if the ball is playable within a water hazard, the player has the full right to attempt to play the ball without penalty. As with other hazards, he may not ground his club before playing the ball. Many a serious golfer has been seen rolling up a trouser leg or donning his waterproofs in an attempt to avoid a penalty stroke. For the less adventurous, it is best to quietly take the punishment for a wayward shot and proceed with the next shot.

A high-walled pot bunker typical of the links courses used in the British Open.

Michelle McGann plays out of a 'splash' bunker typical of parkland courses.

An attempt at a shot out of a water hazard.

THE GREEN

Last stop before the hole, the 'dance-floor' is every golfer's target on approach. The green is all the ground around the hole which has been specifically prepared for putting: it is made up of very fine, closely mown grass which is markedly different to that of the fairway and surrounding rough. The surface is very often undulating, making putting that much more difficult. The 'speed' of the green (referring to how fast the ball rolls) can vary radically between courses depending on type and length of grass, and weather factors. During the actual playing of a hole, the speed of the green may not be tested by rolling a ball on it, or taking a practice putt.

There are many rules governing what a player may do on a green – surprisingly, golfers may chip on the green – but it goes without saying that extra care should be taken to ensure that as little damage as possible is caused in the process of playing to and on it. Pitch marks caused by approach shots should be carefully repaired and care taken not to walk on the players' lines of putts. Many clubs have banned the use of metal spikes on golf shoes due to the damage they cause to the surface of the green.

Once a player's ball lands on any part of the green, he may mark its position, then lift and clean the ball before proceeding with his putt.

The hole

The ultimate destination of any golf ball, the hole is 4in (102mm) in diameter and must be at least 4in deep. If the hole has a lining it must be at least 1in (25mm) below the surface of the green. It is moved around the green from time to time in order to reduce wear and tear to certain parts of the fine grass, and is never placed less than 3ft (1m) from the fringe of the green. The different locations of the hole on the green can change the character of the entire hole (from tee to green), making it easier or more difficult depending on the position in relation to existing hazards.

The flagstick

The flagstick is a movable straight indicator of the position of the hole, and nearly always has some sort of bunting at the top. It is circular in cross-section

Finding the hole: Justin Leonard of the USA putts his way to victory in the 1997 British Open.

A caddie holds the flagstick at a tournament while the golfers putt out.

and its height can vary. The ball is not permitted to hit the flagstick (or its attendant) when it is being attended by a caddy or playing partner for the player or when a stroke is played towards it from on the putting green. If this happens in strokeplay, the player receives a two-stroke penalty; he loses the hole if he is playing matchplay.

Pouring rain calls for patience and a relaxed, methodical approach to the round.

WEATHER CONDITIONS

Golf is a game where there is little protection from weather conditions. Fortunately it can still be played at most times unless the weather is extremely severe – rain is usually not enough to keep the avid golfer off the course, and some brave even snow and sleet to get in a quick 18 holes.

Rain

A golfer will not often admit that he got really wet while playing, even though he may have the appearance of a 'drowned rat'. Protective rain gear is permitted, and an umbrella may be used, however a golfer may not be sheltered by an umbrella held by another person while actually playing a shot. Should he want to (and is dextrous enough), a player may hold the umbrella himself in one hand while playing the stroke with the other.

In competitions, play is seldom cancelled or suspended unless there is a large accumulation of casual water which would render further play grossly unfair. The only time that a player may stop play himself during a strokeplay tournament without fear of penalty is when he believes there is danger from lightning. Because of the relative openness of a golf course, a golfer makes an inviting conductor for lightning, and many unsuspecting players have been struck (American Lee Trevino is a famous example, having been struck while playing in a tournament). Play is usually suspended by means of a siren and restarted by another blast. Players may mark their ball, lift it and then head for safety.

Sun

Ever since the discovery of the hole in the ozone layer and the heightened awareness of the debilitating effects of exposure to the sun and the threat of skin cancer, this has become a major concern to golfers, especially in warmer climates.

Although it is common sense to wear a cap or visor to protect the sensitive skin of the face, it is not widely known that the green grass of a golf course reflects more dangerous ultraviolet (UV) radiation than water. It is therefore advisable to wear a good sunscreen lotion of at least factor 16 to protect oneself from the possible development of skin cancer in later years. When playing 18 holes, golf is almost always played during some of the day's more dan-

Gary Player fending off the rain.

gerous hours, between 11:00 and 15:00, so it is especially important to be adequately protected. An umbrella may be used to shield a player from the sun, but again it may not be held over him while he is playing his stroke.

Most golfers still walk the 4 miles (6km) required to get around 18 holes, so it is important to ensure that one has enough liquids to prevent dehydration on the course on a hot day. Energy is important not only for the swing, but also for the mind that controls it, and any exhaustion will quickly put paid to a good round.

Greg Norman wearing his distinctive 'Great White Shark' headgear as protection against the sun.

Taking things to extremes – golfers will play almost anywhere there is open space and a hole to aim at.

FOUR WAYS TO JUDGE THE WIND

What might seem like a slight breeze where the golfer is standing may turn out to be a howling gale along the ball's intended trajectory or at the green. Check the following before choosing a shot:

Grass test Take a small handful of grass and throw it in front of you, watching how it falls.

Tree tops Look at the upper-most branches of trees along the line of flight to see how the wind is affecting them.

Flag The fluttering flag on the green is a vital indicator of how the wind is affecting your intended target area.

Water Check the ripples on any surrounding water.

Hot, dry deserts make interesting locations for courses.

Wind

Strong wind can turn a relatively easy course into a 'monster' that sends scores soaring. The links courses used for the British Open tournaments are notorious for the howling winds that can sweep across the flat, treeless layouts. Course designers always take prevailing wind patterns into account when designing layouts – often a course looks easy until the golfer has to play it. A good golfer will learn how to cope with wind, whether it is blowing directly into his face or across him. Wind tends to accentuate a bad shot, turning a gentle draw or fade into a wild hook or slice, while a well-struck shot is unlikely to be affected that much. This is probably why hard-hitter Jack Nicklaus was well-known for saying that wind did not affect him.

When playing in strong wind, make sure that clothing and other equipment is secure – should a part of a player's equipment be blown onto his ball, the player would incur a penalty under the Rules and he would have to replace the ball.

Trees blown over in high winds but still attached to the ground are not automatically classified as ground-under-repair; the Club/Tournament Committee can declare them as such at their discretion.

Altitude

Although not a weather factor, it is important to know the altitude at which a course is situated, especially if it is a few thousand feet above sea level. A golf ball travels a lot further at high altitude than it does at sea level and wind has a lesser effect at high altitudes. A golfer can safely bank on his shots going 10 percent further when playing at high altitude and should adjust his club choice accordingly.

Rain with high winds can be a nightmare for a golfer trying to keep his equipment and clothing dry.

43

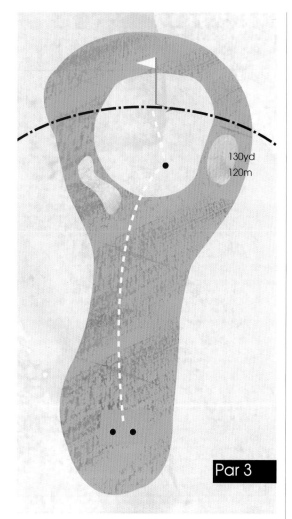

Par 3

A typical par three (above) will require a tee shot that reaches the green and then two putts in order to make par.

THE HOLES: PAR THREES, FOURS AND FIVES
Most 18-hole golf courses have a par of 72, which would usually be made up of four par-threes, four par-fives and 10 par-fours.

Par threes
To reach the green of a par three, it is generally the course designer's intention that golfers play one shot from the tee to the green and then hole out in two putts. Of course, as any average golfer knows, this is seldom the case, which makes these holes particularly testing as there is little room for error. Depending on the skill and strength of the golfer, most par threes are reachable with anything from a pitch-

ing wedge to a medium or long iron depending on the length of the hole. The length can vary vastly from as little as 87yd (80m) to around 219yd (200m).

Par threes are of course the venue (most of the time) of the coveted hole-in-one that every golfer strives for and gains instant fame (or notoriety) for when he achieves it.

Par fours
A tee shot and an approach shot to the green make up the standard method of playing par fours. The most difficult hole on the course will usually be a very long par four which requires a long drive and a

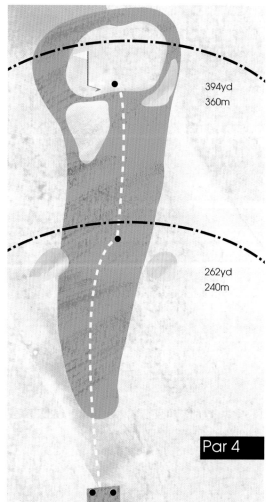

Par 4

Generally, par fours require two shots to reach the green. A two-putt will then ensure a score of level par.

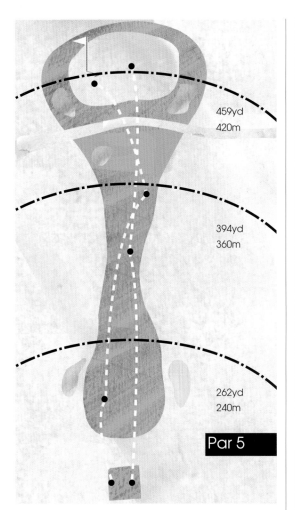

459yd
420m

394yd
360m

262yd
240m

Par 5

The safe approach to a par five is to take three shots to reach the green, but better golfers may attempt to reach the green in two.

The green at the dramatic par four 8th hole at Pine Valley, in New Jersey, USA.

long iron approach. The maximum length for a par four is usually not much more than 440yd (402m) depending on the altitude and slope of the hole. This length is entering par five territory.

Par fives

These are the holes that golfers aim to birdie or par as often as possible because there is always more room for error. Often two excellent shots will be enough to reach the green and set up a possible eagle opportunity. Course designers will often plan for extra hazards around the greens of par fives (in excess of 440yd; 402m) to ensure that only the most fearless of golfers are brave enough to have a go at the green in two shots.

18
PAR 5
548
538

One of the world's most famous par fives, the spectacular 18th hole at Pebble Beach, California.

CHAPTER FOUR

GOLF EQUIPMENT

THE EARLY YEARS

Winston Churchill once said: 'Golf is a game in which you try to put a small ball in a small hole with implements singularly unsuited to the purpose.' There is little doubt that anyone who has experienced the frustrations of golf will agree. Another universal truth is that the money spent on golf equipment today is vast, as is the amount spent on advertising and marketing balls, clubs, shoes, and bags. But the two mainstays of the golf equipment industry remain clubs and balls.

Balls Early golf balls were made of wood, but these were replaced, in the 17th century, by the 'feathery', which owes its name to the fact that it was constructed from boiled feathers stuffed into a small leather bag. This may sound simple, but making a feathery was an art form and the masters of the industry were held in high esteem by the golfing community of the day.

Nobody was better at producing featheries than the Robertson family of St Andrews in Scotland – Allan Robertson was in fact the first person to make a living out of the game. Featheries were expensive items, and they did not last long – a couple of miss-hits from an untalented owner usually meant the end of the ball. The life span was also shortened when the balls were used in wet conditions, as the leather tended to crack when it dried.

But the main reason for the high cost of these balls was the amount of time required to make them. The best craftsmen could only produce up to four a day. It says a lot about the Robertson family that they managed to manufacture in excess of 2000 featheries a year.

The gutta-percha ball (gutty) revolutionized the game in the mid-19th century.

noticed that an old gutty which was pitted and scuffed performed better than a new one, and soon all sorts of patterns were being cut onto new balls, first by hand, later by machine.

Less than 50 years later, the gutty reign was ended by a ball manufactured, almost by accident, of rubber, signalling the dawn of a new era. It was called the Haskell, after its inventor Coburn Haskell. Toying around with rubber bands, he constructed a sphere which fell out of his hand and bounced like nothing he'd ever seen, and a new idea was born. The Haskell was not the most obedient of fliers, but it did travel long distances and led to the lengthening of courses. The problem of an uncontrollable flight path was solved by fitting the ball with a solid outer cover that carried dimple patterns to make it aerodynamic. The dimple pattern and the evolution of golf ball design is an ongoing process today.

Clubs The first golf clubs used in Scotland in the 15th century were wooden implements comprised of a sturdy shaft, a weighted head and a padded handle, bound with leather. It was only in the 18th century that metal-headed clubs made their appearance, eventually taking the place of certain wooden clubs. The 18th and 19th centuries were characterized by the elegant 'play club'. This was a long-nosed, long-shafted, supple driving club designed to give distance off the tee. Golfers also carried a 'grassed driver', a shorter club which had some loft and was used for fairway shots from good lies or to lift the ball when playing downwind. 'Spoons' were shorter clubs with varying loft designed to deal with various

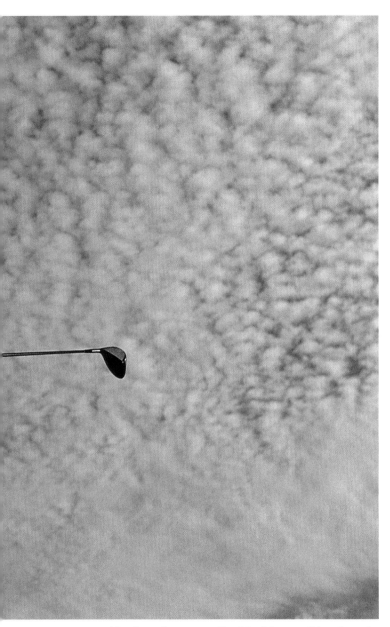

Metal woods are more 'forgiving' than traditional woods.

By the mid-19th century a new product appeared on the market: the feathery made way for the 'gutty', the key ingredient of which was the coagulated and moulded juice of the gutta-percha tree. These were not as expensive as featheries, they lasted longer and could be repaired. The first gutties were smooth and had none of the aerodynamic features found on modern golf balls. As a result, the flight of a new gutty was unpredictable – it dipped and dived rather than travelling straight and true. Players soon

A selection of putters, irons and woods dating back to the early part of the century.

ELEMENTS OF A GOLF CLUB

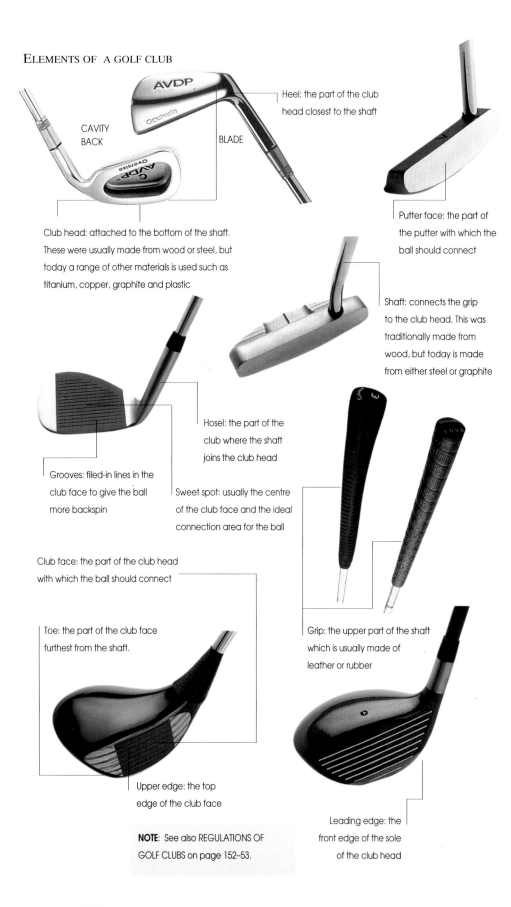

CAVITY BACK

AVDP GOLDWIN

BLADE

Heel: the part of the club head closest to the shaft

Club head: attached to the bottom of the shaft. These were usually made from wood or steel, but today a range of other materials is used such as titanium, copper, graphite and plastic

Putter face: the part of the putter with which the ball should connect

Shaft: connects the grip to the club head. This was traditionally made from wood, but today is made from either steel or graphite

Hosel: the part of the club where the shaft joins the club head

Grooves: filed-in lines in the club face to give the ball more backspin

Sweet spot: usually the centre of the club face and the ideal connection area for the ball

Club face: the part of the club head with which the ball should connect

Toe: the part of the club face furthest from the shaft.

Grip: the upper part of the shaft which is usually made of leather or rubber

Upper edge: the top edge of the club face

Leading edge: the front edge of the sole of the club head

NOTE: See also REGULATIONS OF GOLF CLUBS on page 152–53.

fairway lies. Baffing spoons were designed to remove a piece of turf and produce a high ball flight with little run, while wooden niblicks were well-lofted for getting balls out of the sand. Golfers also carried a wooden putter that was square-faced, with a heavy head.

The arrival of the gutty ball changed club design dramatically – the new ball was harder and heavier, and difficult to control with the slender wooden clubs. As a result, from the late 19th century, wooden club heads became wider and deeper, eventually resulting in the conex-faced 'bulger' driver.

Spoons disappeared, to be replaced by the 'baffy' and 'brassie' which featured a brass striking plate fitted to the sole. Iron clubs were becoming increasingly popular because they were cheaper to manufacture and the gutty could withstand a blow from the iron club face, unlike the feathery.

At the end of the 19th century, a typical set of irons was made up of a driving cleek, iron cleek, lofter, mashie, sand iron, niblick and putting cleek, each with varying degrees of loft. This gradually evolved into the set of irons as we know them today.

Shafts were made of bamboo, ash or hickory – hickory being the most popular. It was only in the 1920s that steel made its appearance in the shaft industry and changed the game forever. Steel was far more consistent and scoring became much easier.

After a long period of steady growth and improvement, the last 20 years have seen an explosion of innovations and refinements in the golf equipment market. Steel has all but replaced wood in the make-up of the distance clubs, and in recent years titanium has also come into the fray. Graphite-shafted clubs are commonplace as are clubs specially designed to meet specific needs of certain groups of golfers.

MODERN GOLF CLUBS
Woods

Ask any golfer about the most satisfying stroke he ever played and he will most likely tell you about a particularly long drive he once powered down the fairway. In the golf equipment industry, the dominance of woods as the top-sellers is unchallenged. Even though woods are used less than all the other clubs in the bag, golfers are prepared to spend enormous amounts of money on them in the search for a few extra yards.

The term 'woods' is still used, despite the fact that the number of clubs actually made of wood is dropping steadily. Steel alloys and titanium are the preferred materials today. 'Metal woods' propel the ball further and are also more forgiving than wooden woods. Even in the case of miss-hits or off-centre connections, the ball still travels some distance and doesn't lose as much accuracy.

Woods are numbered from 1 to 14. The 1-wood is generally known as the driver and is the club which should hit the ball the furthest. Most golfers carry a driver, 3-wood and 5-wood, although better players usually only carry two woods – the driver and a 3-wood – dropping the 5-wood in favour of a long iron or extra wedge. The driver's ability to propel the ball great distances stems from its long shaft and a low-lofted club face. A driver is generally 43–45in (110–114cm) long, although some drivers have shafts of up to 50in (127cm) long. The longer the shaft, the more difficult it is to hit the club consistently well,

While most 'woods' are today made of metal, wooden woods are still produced for traditionalists.

but on well-struck drives the payoff is more distance. The loft on drivers (*see* page 52) ranges from 6.5 to 11 degrees. One of the big advantages of titanium club heads is their ability to get the ball airborne quickly, so titanium-headed drivers generally have less loft than steel- or wooden-headed clubs, but they are significantly more expensive than their steel counterparts. These days, only real traditionalists still carry wooden drivers in their bags.

Modern drivers feature much larger club heads than their predecessors of 20 years ago, yet today's clubs are significantly lighter. The reason for this is the material used in club head manufacture as well as the evolution of graphite shafts. Manufacturers also managed to shave some weight off the grip. This weight loss meant they could design bigger club heads with wider 'sweet spots'.

If you are just starting out, or have trouble hitting your driver well off the tee, consider switching to a 3-wood. It's a versatile club, shorter and more lofted than the driver and therefore easier to use. The 3-wood can also be used to good effect from the fairway. A third wood – normally a 4-wood or a 5-wood – will be even easier to hit from the fairway. These woods are normally referred to as 'utility woods'. Recovery shots from light or even thickish rough are much easier with a utility wood than with a long iron as the wood's club face is better suited to sliding through the grass. Utility woods also have a low centre of gravity, so it is easier to get the ball airborne, and on long approach shots, the ball will often stop quicker on the green.

One final word of advice on the purchase of woods. There is no need for a set of woods to be the same brand or of the same material. More important is to identify your needs and test the ability of different clubs to match your game.

American John Daly is the longest driver on the US PGA Tour.

TYPES OF WOODS

1-wood/driver

3-wood

4-wood

5-wood

7-wood

9-wood

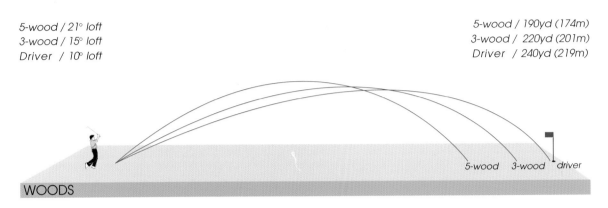

5-wood / 21° loft
3-wood / 15° loft
Driver / 10° loft

5-wood / 190yd (174m)
3-wood / 220yd (201m)
Driver / 240yd (219m)

5-wood   3-wood   driver

WOODS

DISTANCES HIT BY VARIOUS WOODS

3-iron

4-iron

5-iron

6-iron

7-iron

8-iron

9-iron

Irons

Irons are generally used for hitting approach shots. Once you have reached a certain level in the game, you will find that after hitting a decent drive you will require an iron shot to reach the green on a par four. If you are a long hitter, you may even be able to reach the odd par five with an iron on your second shot, but usually your third shot on the long holes will be played with a short iron.

Irons are usually purchased in sets. An average set of irons consists of nine clubs – 3-iron to 9-iron, pitching wedge and sand wedge – and you may also consider getting either an extra long iron (1-iron or 2-iron) or a lob wedge. There is no need for these extra clubs to be of the same make as your set; many golfers do carry long irons and lob wedges that don't belong to their iron-family – it's simply a matter of having tested and liked them.

Each iron sends the ball a different distance. The low-numbered irons are designed to send the ball further, while wedges are generally used from around 110yd (100m) and closer to the green. There is a gap of roughly 11yd (10m) between shots played with each iron, so if you hit your 3-iron 195yd (180m), you will hit a 4-iron 185yd (170m), a 5-iron 175yd (160m) and so on. The longer the iron, the more difficult it is to hit. The long-iron shot is definitely one of the most difficult in the game – and one which few players can hit consistently well.

In the past all irons were designed in a 'bladed' style. Bladed irons are difficult to hit, but the modern oversized cavity-back irons (*see* page 50) have made mastering these clubs much easier. Today, when buying a new set of irons, golfers can choose

Laura Davies, one of the US LPGA Tour's most successful lady golfers, has an accurate short game.

from four design varieties: cast cavity-back, forged cavity-back, cast blade and forged blade. The most popular type is the cast cavity-back which offers golfers the benefits of modern technology – better results from off-centre hits and improved playability in the long irons – at an affordable price. Forged clubs (blades or cavity-backs) are generally more visually appealing than their cast counterparts and manufacturers insist that the forging process produces a higher quality product and improved 'feel' (i.e. they are considered to give a better 'response' on well-struck shots) although they are more expensive. Forged blades remain the benchmark for the better player and are known as 'players' clubs'.

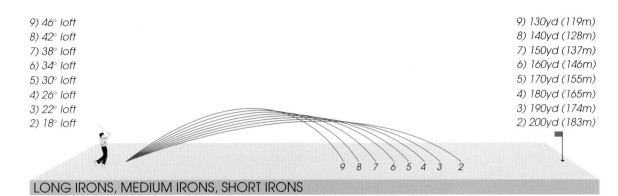

9) 46° loft
8) 42° loft
7) 38° loft
6) 34° loft
5) 30° loft
4) 26° loft
3) 22° loft
2) 18° loft

9) 130yd (119m)
8) 140yd (128m)
7) 150yd (137m)
6) 160yd (146m)
5) 170yd (155m)
4) 180yd (165m)
3) 190yd (174m)
2) 200yd (183m)

LONG IRONS, MEDIUM IRONS, SHORT IRONS

DISTANCES HIT BY VARIOUS IRONS

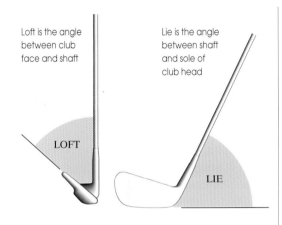

Loft is the angle between club face and shaft

Lie is the angle between shaft and sole of club head

LOFT

LIE

Club heads

The most popular choice of material for club heads in irons is stainless steel, which is less expensive than carbon steel, nickel and other metals. However steel does not give as much feedback, or response, when striking the ball as the 'softer' metals. Titanium is not a favoured material in iron manufacture – it is simply too light and although it offers many advantages and benefits, pure titanium club heads become too big. This has led to a new 'bi-metal' technology in club head design, whereby mass is added to light-weight club heads of titanium by using heavy metals in the sole of the club. The result is a club that has a low centre of gravity and is easy to swing, helping golfers get the ball airborne quickly.

Shafts

For a long time graphite-shafted irons were considered a novelty, but today almost all sets of irons are made with both graphite and steel shafts. Graphite shafts in irons are usually preferred by senior and weaker players as they give added distance, and some players find they offer a better feel than steel shafts. Despite this, steel shafts are still the choice of the masses.

The second half of the 1990s saw some innovative shaft designs in the iron market, and shafts featuring wider tips, bulges and humps have become commonplace. The main aim of these variations is to produce a more stable and consistent club that provides the added benefit of extra distance.

Grip

The grip on a club is generally rubber or leather. As a rule it is not round, but slightly egg-shaped, with a slight ridge at the back of the shaft. It is important to buy clubs with the correct thickness of grip – the fingers of the left hand should just touch the base of the left thumb without digging in.

Your local professional should be able to fit your clubs with new grips to suit you.

Today's shafts are manufactured primarily from steel or graphite. Stiffer shafts suit hard-hitting players while those with more flex are ideal for softer hitters.

Grips to suit all palms and finger widths.

SW) 56° loft
W) 50° loft
9) 46° loft

SW) 80yd (73m)
W) 110yd (101m)
9) 130yd (119m)

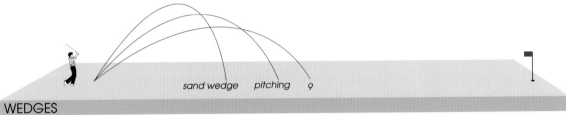

sand wedge   pitching   9

WEDGES
DISTANCES HIT BY WEDGES

Pitching wedge

Sand wedge

The 'Trusty Rusty': wedges made from steel offering better 'feel' have made a return.

Wedges

The late Harvey Penick, one of the greatest teachers the game has known, once said that a man with a good short game is a match for anyone, while a man with a bad short game is a match for no-one. (A short game refers to a golfer's approach shots to the green and putting.)

The average golfer will never get the chance to compete in a Major, but the lesson to be learnt is the same – a good short game will undoubtedly improve your game.

The good news is that modern-day wedges have made this much easier. For a long time the only wedges available on the market were those that formed part of a standard set of clubs; nowadays manufacturers are tapping into the need of a player to improve his short game and virtually all manufacturers offer a separate range of wedges in addition to those issued with their sets.

Standard wedges Two standard wedges form part of every set of clubs: the pitching wedge and the sand wedge. The pitching wedge is generally used for longer approach shots (98–120yd; 90–110m) while the sand wedge is used for shorter shots and for escaping from greenside bunkers.

Gap wedges The gap wedge is designed to be used from a distance at which you would hit your pitching wedge too far and your sand wedge not far enough (the sand wedge should never be forced because when swung hard, it is difficult to control the shot and the ball will simply go higher rather than further). A gap wedge is ideal for those in-between shots. Low-handicap and mid-handicap players usually don't carry a gap wedge, because they learn to

'work' their pitching wedge. However, high handicappers can benefit enormously by carrying one of these wedges – they provide more options and allow you to be more consistent in your swing technique.

Lob wedges The other special wedge – and nowadays the most popular one – is the lob wedge. This is designed for delicate shots around the green and will get the ball airborne quickly due to the high amount of loft on the club.

Loft and bounce Loft is the single most important element in wedge design. Each wedge has a different loft, the pitching wedge having the lowest (46–50 degrees) while the lob wedge has the highest (58–62 degrees).

The second important element in wedge design is the club's 'bounce', the angle between the ground and the sole line of the club when the club is placed on the ground in its natural position and the club's leading edge is perpendicular to the target line. Understanding bounce is not important. On the other hand, it is important to know that it is the bounce that makes clubs easier to use; it causes clubs to glide across the turf rather than dig into it. 'Fat' shots – that is, hitting the ground before the ball – are lessened as a result.

In bunkers, where players are advised to hit the sand rather than the ball, bounce is particularly helpful. The greater the bounce angle, the less the club will dig into the surface and vice versa. Angles of bounce are more beneficial on certain surfaces. On hard surfaces, such as gravel roads, paths and compact sand, you need a small bounce (you want the club to dig rather than to skid), while in bunkers and thickish rough a larger bounce is required.

Design The design style of wedges is still very traditional. Wedges are used for short shots where the feel of contact is important, and nothing provides this better than the more traditional club heads. Also, the benefits that cavity-back clubs bring to wedge play to improve the game are negligible compared to what you lose in feel.

Wedge club heads are made from a variety of materials, including softer metals such as beryllium copper.

Most manufacturers prefer to use softer metals such as nickel, carbon steel or beryllium copper for the club heads of wedges. The reason is obvious: to promote feel. However, these materials wear more quickly than their steel alloy and titanium counterparts, so some manufacturers use face inserts or coatings to prolong the life of the club. The harder material also increases the amount of spin put on the ball by the grooves in the club face.

Putters

The putter is in many ways quite different from other golf clubs. It is the shortest club in the bag, and the only club designed not to launch the ball into the air, but rather to roll it along the grass. The main purpose of the putter is to execute precision shots on the green. It is the club which all golfers will use the most during a round. So if you want to improve your game quickly, work on your putting.

There are more brands and models of putters available on the market than any other golf club.

Putter design can generally be classified into various categories:

Blade This is the classic design. It has a flat club head and is favoured by traditionalists and players who employ an inside-square-inside putting stroke (i.e. players who swing the club freely with their shoulders, opening the blade in the backswing, squaring it up on impact and closing it on the follow-through). The most famous modern player to wield a blade is American Ben Crenshaw. The two-time Masters champion has used the same putter – a Wilson 8802, considered to be a benchmark for blade putters – for virtually his entire career, while fellow American Jack Nicklaus used a blade to win 15 of his 18 Major championships.

Mallet Mallet putters have a distinctive look. The large, rounded head is ideal for the golfer whose stroke takes the putter straight back and through. The main benefit of mallet putters is their face balancing – the combination of the weight distribution in the putter head and the shaft placement gives a neutral and balanced putter face position. Two big-name US putter manufacturers, Ray Cook and Odyssey, have built their empires on successful mallet designs.

Heel-toe This design dominates the market in terms of quantity sold. The heel-toe design puts the bulk of the putter head's weight on the putter's toe and heel. This weight distribution stabilizes the putter head at impact and widens the sweet spot. More events on the US PGA Tour in the last two decades have been won by players using heel-toe putters than any other style of putter. The man who brought heel-toe putters to the fore is Karsten Solheim of the USA, who named the clubs Ping because of the sound they made when they struck the ball. Ping putters still hold the record for the most wins on the world's professional tours. Incidentally, mallet and blade putters can also be heel-toe weighted.

Broom handle These have always been a controversial subject. The broom handle putter is unique for its long shaft and two grips. It is used by golfers who are affected by the 'yips', golfspeak for an attack of nerves that causes twitching, making putting with

Blade putter

Mallet putter

Offset heel-toe putter (made famous by Ping)

Famous 'Bull's Eye' style putter

Putter with milled face

CALAMITY JANE

The great Bobby Jones won the first of his 13 Majors – the 1923 US Open at Inwood Country Club on Long Island, New York – shortly after he had acquired a hickory-shafted blade putter nicknamed Calamity Jane. It was to be the start of a long and beautiful friendship.

The putter came to America from Carnoustie in Scotland in 1903 in the bag of Jim Maiden, a golf professional who found work at Atlanta Athletic Club. There Maiden gave lessons to Jones's parents before leaving to become the pro at Nassau Country Club in New York. Maiden's brother Stewart took over as pro at Atlanta and became Jones's teacher, but Jones still kept in contact with Jim.

The Monday before the 1923 Open, Jones was playing a round at Nassau with Jim and Stewart Maiden and was complaining about his putting. Jim suggested Jones try Calamity Jane, after which Jones promptly holed a 30-footer. That week Jones defeated Bobby Cruickshank in a play-off to win the US Open and went on to win the US Amateur at Merion in 1924, and again in 1925 at Oakmont.

By this time, Calamity Jane's face had become slightly uneven from years of buffing to prevent rust. Jones asked club maker J Victor East to make a copy of the putter and in 1926 East presented Jones with six duplicates. Jones selected one and went on to win his other 10 Majors using Calamity Jane II.

one's hands together virtually impossible. The broom handle is so designed that the golfer's hands work separately so that the twitch can be eliminated. At first this putter was banned by the golfing authorities because it did not conform to existing club regulations. The ban was later overturned, but there has been constant talk of again banning these clubs or laying down certain specifications for the method of gripping the club. The most popular head design used in broom handles is heel-toe.

Putter manufacture As with most other clubs, stainless and carbon steel has been the premier material used in the construction of putters. However, with feel and response being of utmost importance on the greens, manufacturers have successfully experimented with a whole range of different materials and metal alloys.

Experimentation with the putter face has led to two major innovations: face milling and face inserts. Manufacturers believe that a putter with a milled face performs better as the milling process ensures that the putter's face has a consistent, flat surface.

Face inserts became a buzzword in the latter half of the 1990s. By inserting a soft, pliable material in the face of the putter, manufacturers were able to produce a club with an extremely soft feel, because the ball stays on the club face for longer at contact. The result is not only improved response, but also better distance control. The material used differs greatly and these days inserts are made of titanium, aluminium, balata, polymer-based materials and other products.

Loft Many believe that putters have zero degrees of loft, but this is simply not true – putter loft generally fluctuates around the four-degree mark. Putters with more loft

Bernhard Langer has used the broom handle putter effectively to overcome the 'yips'.

will perform better on slow, furry greens, while those with less loft are best used on smooth, fast surfaces. The difference between the most lofted and the least lofted putter is, however, small.

Lie The lie of the putter refers to the way the putter sits on the ground and the angle of the shaft in this position (*see also* page 53). Lie is the most important aspect to look at when buying a putter. It lies correctly when its full sole rests on the ground; aligning the putter then becomes easy. If the toe or heel is off the ground at address, aligning becomes a shot in the dark. Take these factors into consideration when you buy your putter, but ultimately it's a matter of personal preference. Buy one you feel comfortable with and you know will be good for your confidence. Putting is a mind game and using the correct putter could make it much easier.

CLUB HEAD COVERS

One of the best ways to keep your clubs – and your woods in particular – in good condition is to invest in head covers. A set of 14 clubs jostling around in your bag can cause a lot of surface marking. Although iron head covers are available, modern irons can generally withstand being jostled in a bag, but it is woods that really need protection around the head and down onto the shaft. Graphite-shafted clubs are particularly susceptible to scratching.

The covers should be marked – 1, 3 or 5 – so you can easily identify the club. Another important consideration is a good shape that holds well in all weather conditions to ensure a quick, smooth and secure fitting over the club. The ideal shape is a gusset – it's more expensive but it fits better and comes off easily. Avoid fumbling with zips and

The trademark head cover used by Tiger Woods, pictured putting (below left).

buttons. Materials vary – leather is expensive but lasts longer, while PVC is less durable but cheaper. Imitation fur is becoming increasingly popular and has largely replaced sheepskin and suede covers, but these fur covers need to be left off the club to dry if they get wet.

THE GOLF BAG

Until the latter half of the 19th century, golf clubs had always been carried loose under the golfer's arm or by his caddie, and the introduction of the first club car-

Three types of bag: the 'pro bag' (top left), an average golfer's bag (top right), and a stand bag (above).

riers, or golf bag, was a major step forward. Early golf bags were thin, tubular wicker baskets or a wooden tripod supporting a canvas bag with a single handle. By the end of the 19th century, the golf bag had become a vital piece of golfing equipment. The main aim of any

golf bag is to carry a set of golf clubs from point A to point B. All bags are manufactured with this in mind and the ability to safely transport clubs is the most important factor to consider when buying a bag. However, the majority of bags boast many other features to improve your journey around the golf course.

In a standard golf bag you will find two or three smallish pockets in which you can place your glove, tees, balls and valuables. You will also find a bigger pocket – usually on the side of the bag – for the storage of wet-weather garments or sweaters. This pocket also carries the bag's rain cover or hood, which can be fitted to prevent water from running into the bag and wetting the grips if you get caught in a downpour. A critical feature is the carry strap – it should be wide, soft and flexible.

Golf bags come in different shapes and sizes and there are several factors to consider before investing in one. Are you going to carry the bag yourself? Or are you going to employ a caddie or perhaps use a trolley? If you are going to carry it yourself, make sure you buy a light 'carry bag', but if you're going to use a trolley you can consider heavier bags. A stand bag, with collapsible legs, is useful when you need to avoid having to leave your bag lying on wet ground. Check, too, that it has an umbrella holder.

Also make sure the bag you buy will be able to protect your shafts – take a look at the divider in the top of the bag. The best one available is a six-way divider with two horizontal bars and one vertical bar creating six compartments. The divider should have a soft covering to avoid causing scratches and nicks on your shafts.

A bag should be made from durable and waterproof material, otherwise you might find yourself buying a new bag in no time.

The final factor to take into account is appearance. A neat, well-made and fashionable bag not only looks good, but some people believe it actually boosts confidence. Debatable though the theory is, be sure to get full value for your money by giving some thought to the colour you would prefer and the overall appearance of the bag.

Dividers in the neck of the bag should be well-padded to protect club shafts.

Pockets will carry gloves, tees, balls, valuables, and wet-weather gear.

Player's son Wayne shoulders his father's golf bag; with them is Nicklaus.

THE FIRST CADDIES

The word 'caddie' derives from the French 'cadet' which referred to a young man serving in the army forces or at court. Cadets were often used as porters and the local slang term 'caddie' was used to describe the young boys who carried golfers' clubs. These early caddies were expected to select the correct clubs, tee up the ball and attend to the flagstick, plus at all times keep as quiet as possible. Today caddying is a serious profession and the top caddies travel the world with their players and earn substantial fees. In fact, many professional golfers started their careers as caddies.

GOLF CARTS AND TROLLEYS

While all of the top professional golf tours around the world require golfers to walk to their ball, many clubs offer motorized golf carts for hire to amateurs who prefer to ride. Golfers have many reasons for choosing to ride – lack of fitness, to save time, disability, old age (motorized carts are, in fact, allowed on senior professional tours). Motorized carts have a rack on the back for clubs and you will be required to stay on the cart paths around the course. Most golfers prefer to buy or hire a golf trolley or pull-cart as an escape from the tedium of carrying around a heavy golf bag. Battery-assisted pull-carts make it easier to get up those steep hills.

GOLF BALLS

Golf balls come in a bewildering array of prices and brands, but there are essentially three different types, depending on whether they are made from one, two or three pieces.

One-piece balls These are usually the cheapest. They are made of tough, rubberized plastic with a thin surlyn cover, and they are difficult to damage. They are more difficult to control than two- or three-piece balls, however, and don't fly as far. One-piece balls are ideal for beginners who tend

Disabled golfer Casey Martin uses a golf cart on the course.

A pull-cart is an easier alternative to carrying a large bag around the course.

to lose more balls. Driving ranges also make extensive use of this type of ball.

Two-piece balls These cover a good distance and are hardy and easier to control than one-piece balls. The core is made up of a blend of resins that compresses and then expands when hit, to propel the ball further. The thicker surlyn cover makes it difficult to damage. These are used by middle- to high-handicappers for whom distance is usually a priority.

Three-piece balls These have a solid or liquid centre surrounded by high-energy windings. These balls cannot be hit as far as two-piece balls, but they give greater control. The cover is either surlyn or balata,

are generally used by top amateurs and professionals seeking extra control. The balata cover produces greater backspin but is easily damaged if not struck correctly. It is also unfortunately very expensive.

THE GOLF GLOVE

A golf glove ensures a comfortable and secure grip on the club throughout the swing. Right-handers wear a glove on their left hand (and left-handers on their right hand) because it is their dominant hand.

A golf glove should fit like a second skin; it is better to buy one that is a little too tight than one that is too loose. A smaller glove will stretch slightly to fit snugly, while a bigger glove will move around on your hand and prevent you from getting a proper grip. An overlapping Velcro flap round the wrist fastens the glove firmly.

Top-quality leather golf gloves are made from sheepskin that is specially treated to give a softer feel, a better grip and water resistance. Cheaper leather gloves are made of cowhide, which is slightly thicker. Synthetic leather gloves are becoming increasingly popular as they feel almost like leather but last longer

a soft substance that gives superb feel when striking the ball. Surlyn-covered three-piece balls are ideal for single-handicappers who require control rather than distance, while balata-covered three-piece balls

and they are significantly cheaper. These give a good grip in wet conditions, though don't have as soft a feel in dry conditions. An advantage of synthetic leather gloves is that they can be machine washed.

Above *While golf gloves come in a range of colours and materials, a snug fit is the most important factor.*

CASEY MARTIN

The United States Professional Golf Association (US PGA) forbids golfers on its PGA Tour to use motorized carts, claiming that walking is an essential part of the game. However, early in 1998, a talented young golfer, Casey Martin (*see* opposite), who suffers from a severe leg disability that makes it impossible to walk even short distances, took the US PGA to court to get an injunction to allow him to use a cart to play in the secondary Nike Tour (which also falls under the US PGA's jurisdiction). Casey won his case and went on to win the first Nike Tour event of 1998. He became an overnight celebrity and soon afterwards signed a deal with clothing and footwear manufacturer Nike to be part of an ad campaign titled 'I can'.

GOLF BALL STRUCTURE

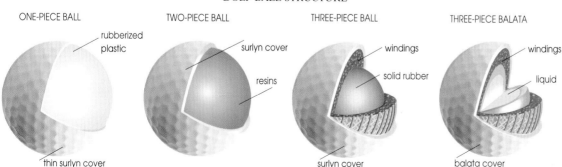

ONE-PIECE BALL — rubberized plastic — thin surlyn cover

TWO-PIECE BALL — surlyn cover — resins

THREE-PIECE BALL — windings — solid rubber — surlyn cover

THREE-PIECE BALATA — windings — liquid — balata cover

Above *Essential golfing accessories (from left): ball markers, spare shoe spikes, spike spanner, pencil, pitch mark repairers, sponger, and tees.*

Opposite *Typically, a set of clubs for a beginner would be made up of three woods (1, 3, 5), nine irons (3 to a sand wedge) and a putter.*

Above right *A comfortable rain suit is essential for wet weather.*

Below *Typical golfing apparel – golf cap, golf shirt, light long pants and golf shoes.*

THE SMALL ACCESSORIES

Before setting out for a round of golf, there are a number of small accessories you will need to make your round smoother:

• Tee pegs: on which to tee the ball up when you drive. These were traditionally made of wood but plastic tee pegs are common today.

• Ball marker: use a purpose-made ball marker or a small coin to mark your ball on the green if it is in the way of your partner's ball.

• Pitch repairer: this is used to repair the pitch mark your ball makes when it lands on the green.

• Sponger: to clean dirt from the golf ball.

• Towel: for drying down the grip and face of your clubs on a wet day or for wiping clean a golf ball.

• Pencil: for writing the score on the scorecard.

• Bag: take your car keys, wallet, and so on out of your pockets before you start your round, placing them in a small bag and then into a pocket in your golf bag. This prevents them from rattling around or getting lost.

• Spare spikes: spikes sometimes work themselves loose from the sole of a golf shoe during a round. In your bag, carry a couple of spare spikes and a small tool to fit them.

GOLFING APPAREL

Clothing

A golfer's clothing should not only be neat and tidy and in keeping with the rules of the club, it should also be practical and comfortable. Your clothes should allow free movement of those parts of your body that are essential to the basic shots. Bear in mind that you will be out on the course for several hours, during which there could be changes in the weather, so be prepared – make sure you can keep warm and dry.

Dealing with the weather

• Wet-weather gear: if the weather conditions indicate the possibility of rain, make sure you have a good golf umbrella with you out on the course. A fibreglass model is safer if lightning is common in your area. Take several pairs of gloves in case one gets soaked. Hang your towel inside the umbrella to keep it dry so you can wipe down the grips of

your clubs. Cover the top of your bag with a hood to keep your clubs dry. A set of full waterproofs – a lightweight jacket and over-trousers – will enable you to keep playing in wet weather yet will not greatly interfere with your swing. Choose a fabric that will allow your skin to 'breathe' and release any perspiration.

• A hat or cap is essential – choose a waterproof hat if the weather is bad. With the increasing number of cases of skin cancer, some sort of protective covering is obligatory in sunny weather, as is a good, non-greasy sunscreen.

Shoes

Golf shoes have several purposes, but are worn primarily to secure a steady stance when hitting the ball and they keep your feet dry and comfortable over four hours of walking. What sets golf shoes apart from regular sports shoes, sneakers or running shoes

Golf shoes showing the difference between 'soft' spikes (top) and metal spikes (bottom).

is their studded soles. Metal or rubber spikes (cleats) give stability and grip. For many years, metal spiked shoes were undoubtedly the leader in the golf shoe industry, but shoes with plastic or 'soft' cleats are fast making inroads into the market. There are several reasons for this rise in popularity, the most important of which is that they don't damage putting surfaces. Metal spikes penetrate the surface of the green, lifting blades of grass and leaving 'spike marks', which also results in the spread of alien grasses and weeds onto greens. As a result, many clubs in the USA and around the world are forcing players to wear plastic cleats.

Rubber-studded shoes are also lighter and easier on your feet, plus you're allowed to wear them into the clubhouse, something you can't do when wearing metal spikes because of the damage caused to carpets and wooden floors. Metal spikes do, however, give superior traction.

When buying a pair of shoes, take the following into account. First, the all-important and basic function of traction: without good traction you will not make consistent contact with the ground and your scores will suffer. If you frequently play in wet conditions, make sure you buy a pair of waterproof shoes – there is nothing more irritating to a golfer than wet feet.

The appearance of your shoes is also important: choose a colour that goes with your clothing and keep in mind that it is easier to maintain dark-coloured shoes than a light-coloured pair.

Finally, the price range. Although they are expensive, top-of-the-range shoes are worth the cost outlay because they are well made and will give you everything you need in a golf shoe. So if you are a golf 'nut', the investment in a good pair will definitely pay its dues. If you're a social golfer, look for a pair that offers you most of the benefits for a lower price.

The best way to save money on golf shoes is to look after your current pair; you will get fine service from them for up to three years.

CHAPTER FIVE

HOW TO PLAY

Golf is not a game that can be perfected. Through the ages, some have come close to having 'the perfect swing' or the 'perfect putting stroke', but there is no-one who can really claim to be the perfect golfer.

One can safely say that almost every golfer, even the top professional, is looking to improve some aspect of his game, and very few golfers will ever be satisfied with their achieved level. Everyone looks to improve. This can only be done through practice. The best manuals, videos or teaching aids will never provide all the answers. Solutions lie on the practice range, or on the course itself.

The fundamental keys to a good golf swing have very little to do with the swing itself, but rather with a good starting point: the grip, the stance and alignment. More than 80 percent of all faults can be traced back to approaching one of these three factors poorly. They are covered in depth in this chapter, and it is a worthwhile exercise to constantly refer to this section before going out to practise or to play a round – or even afterwards when trying to diagnose a fault.

A word of warning, though: do not be overanalytical, unless of course you are prepared to spend countless hours on the practice range, working on minor aspects of your swing.

It pays to visit an experienced teaching professional who can give you pointers on those elements of your swing that can improve your game and thus make it more enjoyable for yourself. Avoid the pro who promises to make you the next world-beater in one or two lessons – or with a couple of swing tips. This is unlikely to happen.

"IF I'M ON THE COURSE AND LIGHTNING STARTS, I GET INSIDE FIRST. IF GOD WANTS TO PLAY THROUGH, LET HIM."

— BOB HOPE

Scotland's Colin Montgomerie has dominated the game in Europe for half a dozen years.

Lastly, try to make any practice you engage in count (it can – and should be – enjoyable). The practice range is not the place to see how quickly you can scatter 100 balls around the park. Use the time carefully, and after having set yourself sensible targets, walk away feeling that you have achieved something. Practise each target one at a time until you have mastered that particular technique. Use Gary Player's exercises and drills later in this chapter to help you achieve better golf.

THE GOLF SWING

A successful golf swing is built on five fundamentals: grip, addressing the ball, posture, aim and alignment, and ball position. We will deal firstly with these five essential elements, before providing a step-by-step breakdown of the basics of a sound golf swing.

THE BASIC GRIPS

In order to be able to swing the club with control and speed you will need to hold the club securely, but without muscle tension, and ensure that the club face is square at impact. A correct grip is vital for control of the club face and in turn the ball. Many different ways of holding a golf club have been tried and tested over the years, but today there are three basic grips that are used by most golfers.

The overlapping grip

The overlapping grip, also known as the Vardon grip, is the most commonly used and is the best for most golfers except those with small hands. To hold a club using the overlapping grip (*see* 1–7 below): First rest the grip of the club diagonally across the palm of the left hand so that it falls across your hand from heel to the middle of your forefinger. Close your hand around the grip so that it falls in the bend of your forefinger and wrap your fingers lightly – not tightly – around it. You will find that your thumb lies on the right of the top of the club handle and the V-shape formed by your thumb and forefinger points towards your right shoulder. Now place the right hand beneath the handle such that the club shaft rests in the bend of the middle two fingers, not at the base of the fingers.

Now for the overlap (*see* 5–7 below): place the little finger of the right hand over the knuckle of your left forefinger. Close the right hand's thumb and forefinger around the grip such that the V-shape formed by your right thumb and forefinger also point to your right shoulder. Don't grip the club too far down or too near the top; ideally, about 1in (2–3cm) of the end of the club should be visible.

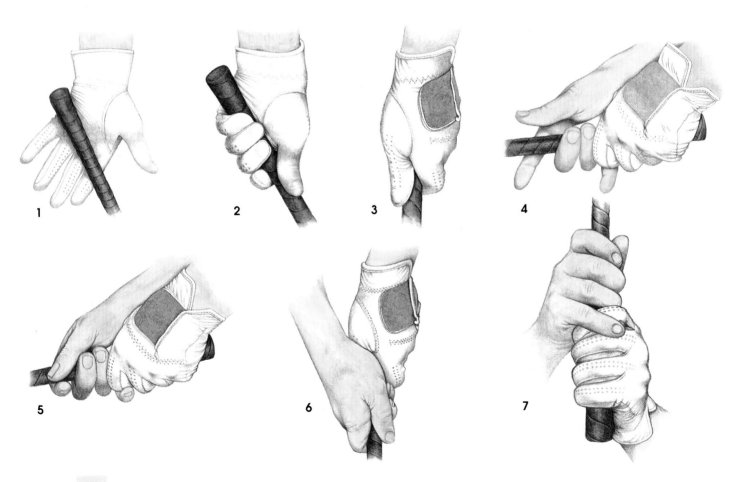

1

2

3

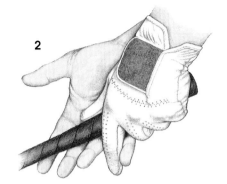

4

The interlocking grip

Many amateurs use this grip and it is ideal for golfers with weak grips or small hands. Place the grip diagonally across the palm of your left hand, but keep your left forefinger outstretched, pointing downwards. Place the right hand beneath the left one and slip the left forefinger between the last two fingers of the right hand. Rest the club shaft in the bend of the middle two fingers of the right hand and close the right hand around the handle. The left thumb will be covered by the right hand. Make sure that you keep your grip firm but not rigid.

The two-handed, baseball or 10-finger grip

This grip is used by juniors and adults with small hands. Hold the club with the left hand using a 'pistol'-like grip – all four fingers are wrapped around the handle and the thumb is on top and just to the right. Now move the right hand up against the handle, keeping your right palm facing the

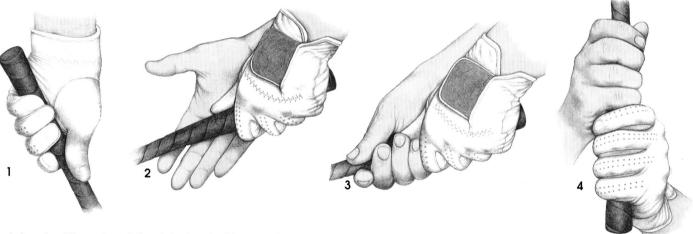

1

2

3

4

left palm. The palm of the right hand will cover the thumb of the left hand. Wrap all four fingers of the right hand around the grip with your thumb on top, such that your right hand's little finger lies snugly up against, but not overlapping, your left forefinger.

Weak and strong grips

The position of your hands on the grip will determine whether you have a weak or a strong grip. In a **weak grip**, only one knuckle of your left hand is visible when you hold the club, forcing your body to aim left. Both Vs in your hands now point more to the left. This will result in a 'fade' – a left-to-right movement of the ball in the air. In a **strong grip**, three knuckles of your left hand are showing, forcing the body alignment to aim right and resulting in a 'draw' or right-to-left ball movement in the air. A **neutral grip** will have two knuckles of the left hand showing.

WEAK GRIP

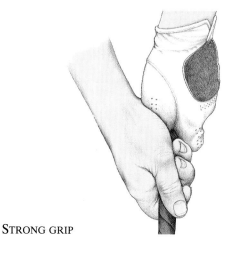

STRONG GRIP

Sam Snead's famous analogy for gripping a golf club – the grip should be firm but not tight.

It's important not to grip the club too tightly. Your grip must be firm, but not so tight that it causes tension in your wrists and forearms. Legendary golfer Sam Snead came up with a famous comparison: hold the club as if you were holding a baby bird.

ADDRESSING THE BALL

Before taking up position in front of the ball, take the time to do a short orientation routine: survey the layout of the hole you are about to play, taking in the terrain, the lie, hazards, the length of the hole, as well as outside influences such as the wind. Visualize the shot you are about to play, think of where you would like the ball to go. You are now

Right and above right
Correct posture is essential to achieving a successful golf swing.

ready to address the ball, which involves getting your body into the correct posture and alignment towards the target, and in relation to the ball.

POSTURE

First, stand straight up in front of the ball. Bend over but from the hips, not the waist, keeping your spine straight. Flex your knees slightly, enough to keep you balanced when swinging. Keep your head on the same plane as the spine, not tilted forward or to the left or right. Your eyes should look straight ahead and your chin should be kept out from the chest, not tucked in, to allow room for your shoulders to turn.

The right hand is positioned lower on the club, so the right shoulder will be slightly lower than the left at address. The hands should be in line with the club head (although this changes for short irons when the hands may be angled towards the target to produce a descending blow. The arms should hang down freely from the shoulders.

If you are using a driver, your stance should be wide enough for your heels to be shoulder-width apart. Reduce the width of your stance as the clubs become shorter. The right foot should be positioned at right angles to the target line (although if you're not that flexible you can turn your right foot outwards to allow a proper shoulder turn). The left foot should be positioned slightly to the left.

The distance you stand away from the ball will obviously vary depending on the length of the club you are using. To find the correct distance for each club, hold the club out in front of you, flex your knees and bend from the hips, lowering the club until the club head touches the ground and the shaft is at 90 degrees to your spine.

AIM AND BODY ALIGNMENT

This three-step routine will help you find the correct alignment:
• First, grip the club in your hand and orientate towards the target (look at where you are hitting).
• Then align the club face so that its bottom edge is facing square towards the target.
• Finally, align your body at right angles to the edge of the club. Feet, knees, hips and shoulders must all

CORRECT BODY ALIGNMENT

Three steps to correct alignment: look at the target first (left); align the club face towards the target (below left); step into position and take up your stance correctly aligned towards the target (below).

be aligned with the club face, on a line parallel to the target line. A classic image to use is to imagine yourself standing on a set of railway tracks leading straight towards the target, with your feet placed on the inside rail and the club face aligned squarely with the outside rail.

A 'closed' body position (in which the body is aligned to the right of the target) will produce a right-to-left ball movement, i.e. a draw, or hook. An 'open' alignment will produce a left-to-right ball flight, i.e. a fade, or slice.

BALL POSITION

When using a driver, the longest club, the ball should be aligned opposite your left heel. As the clubs get shorter, the ball moves back in your stance.

Above *Ball position for a driver (right); for a 5- or 6-iron (centre); and for a wedge (left).*

For a medium iron (a 5- or 6-iron) the ball should fall midway between your left heel and the centre of your stance, while for wedge shots the ball should be positioned midway between your heels.

THE SWING

Once you have taken up the proper stance, the golf swing begins with the 'takeaway', a smooth and controlled movement. For the first 18in (45cm), the club head should move straight back away from the ball along the target line, the left shoulder, left arm and club shaft moving together. Thereafter the club head follows the turning of the hips and shoulders. Never rush: a smooth takeaway will set a proper tempo for your swing and allow a wide arc.

When the shaft reaches the point where it is parallel to the ground, it should point directly along the target line, your left arm should be fully extended but not rigid, your right arm should be bent and relaxed. To understand the path the club should take on the backswing, visualize Ben Hogan's classic image of a pane of glass that extends at an angle from the ball up to your shoulders, and has a hole for your head. As your arms pass your hips, they should remain just below and parallel to the angle of the pane of glass throughout the backswing; this will prevent your backswing from becoming too steep or too flat. As the backswing gets underway, your body weight should start to shift over the right foot, and your head will move sideways to the right. Your right leg should stay flexed throughout the backswing. Although your weight shifts to the right it's important not to sway during the backswing.

Instructor Percy Boomer used his own classic image to help his pupils understand this. He told them to imagine being in a barrel that extends from the chest to the knees, big enough to allow one's hips to turn but not big enough to allow them to sway forwards or backwards. When the club head reaches the top of the backswing, most of your weight should be over your right foot, your hips have turned about 45 degrees, your shoulders about 90 degrees and your back will be facing the target.

PERCY BOOMER'S 'BARREL' IMAGE
OF A PERFECT BACKSWING

Takeaway.

Backswing.

At the top.

Downswing.

Impact.

Follow-through.

Finish.

Your left knee has folded to the right. At this point the shaft of the club should be horizontal, with the club head pointing directly at the target.

The downswing begins with your left knee and hip turning towards the target, which starts to shift the weight back to your left side. Drop your right shoulder and arm straight down, towards your right hip. It's important not to rush the downswing, but to accelerate the club head smoothly. Use Hogan's image of a pane of glass to understand the correct plane – the difference is that on the downswing the plane is flatter and aligned a little to the right of the target. The club head picks up speed quickly during the downswing as the body uncoils.

At impact the centrifugal force created by the body turning around the spine will uncock your wrists and straighten your left arm as the club face makes contact with the ball, while the left hip and shoulder have turned towards the target. The body weight has now shifted over the left foot.

The follow-through and finishing position are as important as the backswing and downswing – virtually the entire weight is now over the left foot, while the right foot has come up so that only the toes are resting on the ground. Shoulders, hips and knees are level and you should be perfectly balanced. You should finish by facing the target with the club over your left shoulder.

Following pages *Looking across the par three 11th hole of the Talon Course at Grayhawk Golf Club in Scottsdale, Arizona, USA.*

WARM-UP ROUTINE

The golf swing is a relatively quick movement that requires good muscle co-ordination. As in any sport, it is advisable to warm up and stretch the relevant muscle groups – and give your mind a chance to get attuned to the game before hitting your first shot. The warm-up may seem unnecessary for the short game (putting, chipping, pitch shot), but it *is* a preventative measure against muscle aches and strains.

GARY PLAYER'S WARM-UP EXERCISES

Turn Head
Turn head to right and to left.

Lift Club over Head
Place a club on the ground in front of your feet. From an upright standing position, bend forward from the hips, keeping the knees slightly bent, and pick up the club. Using straight arms, lift the club over and behind your head and reverse the movement until the club is on the ground again. Repeat 15 times.

Tilt Club Sideways
Hold the club with both hands above the head, arms straight, feet hip-width apart. Bend to the right and to the left for a sideways stretch. Repeat 15 times.

Club Behind Shoulder

Using both hands, hold the club behind the neck and across the shoulders, with knees slightly bent and feet hip-width apart. Twist your torso to the right and left. Repeat 10 times.

Stretch Back Muscles

Place the club head on the ground with the club shaft pointing straight up. Using the club as an upright support, stretch your back while straightening your arms parallel to the ground. Hold this position for the count of 10. Alternate from the upright position to the stretch position. Repeat five times.

Jump with Hip Twist

Hold a club in each hand in a vertical position. The body is positioned in the middle with feet together. Jump, turning the body from the hips, keeping the feet together, to as far right and then as far left as you can. Start slowly, and repeat 10 times.

W A R M - U P

77

Backward Lunge
Hold a club in a vertical position in each hand, with feet together, slightly behind the clubs. Move the right foot straight back as far as possible, with the knee just off the ground, while the left knee bends at an angle of 90 degrees. Hold the upper body as upright as possible. Do the same movement with the other leg. Repeat five times.

Swing with Two Clubs
Grip two golf clubs together and swing very slowly, imitating your normal swing pattern as closely as possible. Increase the speed of the swing after 10 repetitions for a further 10 swings. Repeat 20 times.

PRACTICE

When practising, it is most beneficial to your game to start with the shorter clubs and shots, building up to the full swing with the driver last. This gives both your mind and your body a chance to focus on all the fundamentals of the swing. That is not to say that the following advice is the only way to practise. It is a guide and every golfer should do what he or she is comfortable with.

THE CHIP SHOT

With this shot the flight of the ball in the air is extremely short, followed by a long, calculated and controlled roll on the smooth surface of the green up to the hole. It is used to hit the ball over the fringe to land on the putting area.

Grip   For greater control, grip the club lower down with the right thumb touching the right forefinger. After addressing the ball, you should see two knuckles of the left hand, and the two Vs formed by your thumbs and forefingers should point more or less to your right shoulder. You should grip the club mainly with the last three fingers of the left hand and the middle and second last finger of the right hand. Some golfers choose to use the reverse overlap grip that they use for putting, which gives them more control and reminds them that the swing should be similar to the putting stroke.

Stance The feet are hip-width apart with slightly more weight on the left foot. Feet, hips and shoulders are parallel to the target line, while some more advanced players may point the feet slightly towards the target. The club head is placed behind the ball with the sole of the club evenly on the ground; the club's leading edge is square to the hole. The ball lies in the midpoint between the feet. The club is held low down on the grip, with the club shaft an extension of the straight left arm. The right arm is slightly bent and the head is slightly ahead of the ball.

Swing The swing is very similar to that of the putting stroke: the club should be swung back and towards the hole along the target line, keeping the club face square to the hole. After completing the swing, the left wrist should be in line with the back of the left hand and forearm, and the club face should point towards the target. Not only the wedge but almost any iron can be used for the chip shot, depending on the length of flight required and the distance the ball should roll to the hole. It is often easier to get the ball on the green as quickly as possible and let it run to the hole. The average golfer is likely to achieve better results, therefore, by trying a longer club like an 8- or 7-iron rather than a wedge or sand wedge when faced with a longish chip shot.

GARY PLAYER'S CHIP SHOT PRACTICE AND GAMES

Throw a Ball to the Hole
Aim of exercise Adjusting the speed and extension of your arm movement to the distance the ball has to travel.
Throwing a ball gives you a feeling of where it has to drop first before rolling to the hole.

"I CAN'T EMPHASIZE ENOUGH HOW IMPORTANT A SHARP SHORT GAME IS FOR A GOLFER. SOME 70 PERCENT OF ALL GOLF SHOTS ARE PLAYED FROM 16 YARDS IN TO THE FLAG AND A LARGE PERCENTAGE OF THESE ARE SAND SHOTS. TO UNDERLINE THIS POINT, LET'S TAKE A PLAYER WITH A 14 HANDICAP AND GIVE HIM SOME HELP IN THE SHAPE OF TWO CONSIDERABLE PLAYERS: JOHN DALY AND COREY PAVIN. IF DALY HIT EVERY DRIVE FOR THE 14 HANDICAPPER, WHO THEN TOOK OVER TO PLAY THE OTHER SHOTS IN EVERY HOLE, THAT HANDICAPPER WOULD FINISH AT, SAY, 10 OVER PAR. BUT IF THE 14 HANDICAPPER HIT EVERY DRIVE AND EVERY SECOND SHOT AND PAVIN PLAYED FOR HIM WITHIN 60 YARDS OF THE GREEN, HE WOULD FINISH AT ABOUT THREE OVER PAR. THAT'S FOOD FOR THOUGHT." — *GARY PLAYER*

Chip with an Extra Long Club
Aim of exercise Leading the left arm while keeping firm wrists.
For this exercise you need to construct an extension of approximately 24in (60cm) onto your club shaft. The extended club shaft will force you to keep your left wrist firm, and hands ahead of the ball on the follow-through. If you fail, you'll feel it in the ribs!

Hit Ball with Eyes Closed

Aim of exercise Concentrating on the correct swing movement.

Close eyes after addressing the ball, and swing the club back and towards the target.

Hit a Paper Plate

Aim of exercise Experiencing different ball flights with different clubs.

Try to hit the paper plate (adjusting the height on the pin, or flagstick). Swing different clubs to find out which one will produce the required height.

Chip over a Golf Bag

Aim of exercise Trying out different ball flights using different clubs.

Place the golf bag in your target line as an obstacle. Hit the ball over the golf bag without touching it. Adjust your club selection by moving the bag backwards and forwards.

THE PITCH SHOT

After practising the chip shot extensively, it will be clear to you that only a limited distance and ball height can be achieved by using a firm left arm and wrist movement. To be able to play over hazards such as bunkers or water to a fairly tight pin position, you need to be able to hit the ball higher and subsequently stop it quicker on the green.

Swing Concept

Swing the hands back just above hip-height by cocking the wrists early until the club shaft points to the sky. Reverse the motion with the club back towards the ball by pulling down with the left arm, and hit the ball with a square club face. You should finish with the club head fairly low after impact.

Practice aid Place a club in front of your feet parallel to the target line; place a second club square to the first club opposite the ball.

Grip The grip should be exactly the same as for the chip shot and the club should once again be held low down on the grip.

Stance The club should be placed behind the ball in the same way as for the chip shot, but the ball should be positioned further forward, opposite the inside of the left foot. The feet should be approximately hip-width apart with about 60 percent of your weight on the left foot. Your feet, hips and shoulders should be parallel to the target line and your left foot positioned at approximately 45 degrees to the target line. Your head should be more or less in line with the ball. Bend your knees slightly more than for the chip shot. Remember that the club shaft is an extension of the left arm.

Backswing Swing the hands back just above hip-height by cocking your wrists early until the club shaft points to the sky. The right elbow should be slightly bent. It is vital to keep the head still throughout the swing. The elbows should be kept the same distance apart as during the address position and knees should remain bent. Keep your feet firmly on the ground with little, if any, transfer of weight.

Follow-through With a reverse motion of the club back towards the ball, and keeping the left arm straight, hit the ball square with the club face. Keep the hands in line with the club head and finish as low as possible. On completion of the swing, the hands and club head should be one line, and the back of the left hand and club face should face the target.

GARY PLAYER'S PITCH SHOT EXERCISES AND GAMES

Practice Around an Elevated Green
Aim of exercise Adapting your swing to the required ball height and distance.
Practise the described swing onto an elevated green using a pitching wedge.

Obstacle Game

Aim of exercise Choosing the right club for different heights and distances. A group of players nominate different obstacles to play over (e.g. small tree, bunker, water hazard, golf bag) towards the green, trying to land their balls as close as possible to the hole. The ball should be holed out and the player with the least number of shots wins a point.

THE HALF-SWING

Now that the chip and pitch shots have been extensively practised, it is time to move onto focusing on swinging the club by building up from a half-shot through to the full swing. The half-swing will result in a higher shot than the chip shot, but with as much roll on the ball. For the half-swing, the hands in the backswing and follow-through should reach no higher than hip-height.

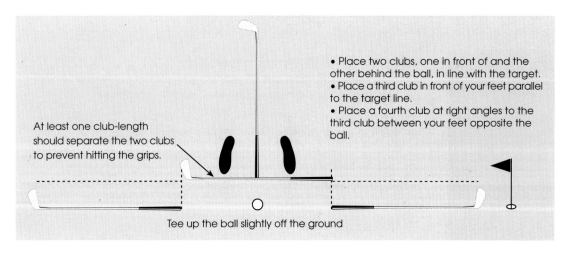

At least one club-length should separate the two clubs to prevent hitting the grips.

• Place two clubs, one in front of and the other behind the ball, in line with the target.
• Place a third club in front of your feet parallel to the target line.
• Place a fourth club at right angles to the third club between your feet opposite the ball.

Tee up the ball slightly off the ground

Practice aid *See* illustration left. Ideally you should practise the half-swing with a 7- or 8-iron. The address and club position – and the grip – are the same as for the chip shot, but hold the club higher up in the normal position. The ball should lie at the midpoint between the feet, set just over hip-width apart. Your weight should be evenly balanced on both feet.

Stance Feet, hips and shoulders should once again be parallel to the target line. Your left arm and club are one straight line and your head is slightly behind the ball. Keep your head in line with your spine and your knees slightly bent. To check your body posture, place the club along your spine so that the surface of your spine and back of your head touch the club. Bend forward slightly from the hips and let your arms hang down loosely. Allow enough room to swing in front of the body.

Backswing With a straight left arm and a progressive turn of the left forearm (pronation), swing the club back so that it finishes parallel to the ground and also to the target line. The right elbow bends slightly, but keep your elbows close together. Keep your head in line with the ball, using the spine as a vertical axis around which the shoulders and hips turn. At the peak of the backswing your hands will be no more than hip-height and your belt buckle and hands will face each other. The club face will have opened up to 90 degrees from its initial position (pronation). Keep knees bent and feet firmly on the ground. Your weight should have transferred to the inside of the right foot.

Downswing and follow-through Keeping the left arm straight, with a reverse turn of the left forearm (supination), the club face moves back into a square impact position. After impact the right arm straightens and starts to roll over the left arm until you get into the same hip-high position as on the backswing. Keep the head in line with the ball, using the spine as a vertical axis, turning shoulders and hips. The club shaft is now parallel to the ground and to the target line. At the finish position your hands will not be more than hip-high and your belt buckle and hands will again face each other. To get the required hip turn, lift the right heel off the ground by turning the right instep inwards as the weight transfers to the left foot. After the follow-through you should be able to see your left palm.

GARY PLAYER'S HALF-SWING EXERCISES AND GAMES

Beachball Swing

Aim of exercise Visualizing and feeling the correct movement.
For the half-swing: from address position through the back-swing to the finish position, a selected colour (e.g. red) on your beachball should constantly point upwards.

Swing with Left Arm Only

Aim of exercise Becoming aware of a controlled club movement with the left arm. Swing the club with your straight left arm backwards and forwards along the target line by rotating your left forearm so that the left thumb is parallel to the ground at the top of the backswing and follow-through.

Tee-to-tee Exercise

Aim of exercise Practising the correct turn of the left forearm and grooving the correct club path.

Place a tee into the top of the club grip of your 8-iron. Tee up the ball. Swing hands back, turning the left forearm until the tee in the club grip points towards the teed-up ball. After hitting the ball by turning the left forearm into the follow-through, end up with the tees once again pointing towards each other.

Distance Game

Aim of exercise Practising the swing using different clubs for varying distances.

Using the suggested range of clubs (sand wedge up to 7-iron), practise the half-swing by aiming at targets placed about 22yd, 44yd, 66yd (20m, 40m and 60m) from you.

THE THREE-QUARTER SWING

In the three-quarter swing, the hands in the backswing and follow-through reach shoulder-height. The three-quarter swing can be played using a sand wedge and any club up to a 5-iron.

The grip and the set-up are exactly the same as for the half-swing, but the ball position does change slightly as you use different clubs. The longer the club, the further away the ball is from your feet and the more the ball should be addressed towards your left foot. For the shortest club, place the ball opposite the midpoint of the feet. Your stance should widen a bit from your regular one with your feet nearly shoulder-width apart.

Stance Feet and shoulders should be parallel to the target line. The left foot is facing outwards, approximately 45 degrees to the target line. Your body posture should be the same as for the half-swing.

Backswing Aim for precisely the same club path as the half-swing, but this time continue to raise the hands to shoulder-height. Keep the left wrist in a straight line with the fore-arm and the back of the left hand. The left thumb should face slightly backwards and up to the sky. At the top of the three-quarter backswing there must be an approximate 90-degree angle between the club shaft and left forearm; the right elbow points towards the ground. Hips and shoulders turn while the head remains relatively still. Keep both knees bent and both feet on the ground and again transfer weight to the inside of the right foot.

Follow-through Swing the club into the impact position by reversing the backswing. Roll the fore-arms as you continue the follow-through, keeping the elbows close together. At the top of the three-quarter follow-through there must be an approximate 90-degree angle between the club shaft and the left forearm, and the left thumb should face slightly backwards and up to the sky. The left wrist is in a straight line with the left forearm and the back of the left hand. At the same time, the left elbow should be pointing to the ground. It is necessary to turn the hips more than you do in previous shots in order to keep your belt buckle and hands facing each other.

GARY PLAYER'S THREE-QUARTER SWING EXERCISES AND GAMES

Swing Bucket

Aim of exercise Getting an overall feeling of the arm movement by swinging the bucket.

With straight arms held out and palms facing each other, grasp the bucket. Using a slight turn of the forearms, swing the bucket sideways and upwards to shoulder-height. In the follow-through, keep the arms straight and swing the bucket sideways and upwards to reach the same position as in the backswing.

Swing with Left Arm Only

Aim of exercise Becoming aware of a controlled club movement with the left arm.

With a straight left arm, swing the club backwards and forwards towards the target by turning your left forearm so that the left thumb faces the sky at the top of the backswing and follow-through.

Target Shots

Aim of exercise Ensuring the correct club selection for varying distances.

Practise hitting at a target using the three-quarter swing. Try out different clubs to reach different targets at the same time maintaining a constant swing tempo.

THE FULL SWING

Having practised the three-quarter shot, you are ready to take a full swing and get the maximum distance with your chosen club. Now practise with the longer clubs (the 4-iron up to the driver) because these clubs, having less loft, need maximum club head speed to get the ball into the air. An extension of the three-quarter swing, make sure you get your hands to around head-height in the backswing and follow-through. Use the same practice aid as for the half-swing.

Ball position The ball should be more or less in line with the left heel.

Stance Feet are shoulder-width apart and the head is slightly to the right of the ball. For long irons and fairway woods, the weight is evenly balanced on both feet. To tee up a ball for a wood shot, measure the depth to which you push in the tee so that half of the ball appears above the top edge of the chosen wood. Approximately 60 percent of your weight is on the right foot.

Backswing Turn your hips horizontally (approximately 45 degrees) and your shoulders 90 degrees to their initial address position. At the top of the backswing the left thumb and club shaft should be parallel to your target line and the ground. Swing hands just above the head. Keep both knees bent, and transfer your weight to the inside of the right foot.

Follow-through Swing the club into the impact position by reversing the backswing; start the swing by pulling down your left arm. The hands finish at approximately head-height. The left wrist remains in a straight line with the forearm and the back of the left hand (the left forearm acts as an upright support for the club). Your belt buckle and body front are facing parallel to the target. Transfer your weight to the outside of the left foot. Check that your hands finish the swing with a firm grip.

P
R
A
C
T
I
C
E

GARY PLAYER'S FULL-SWING EXERCISES AND GAMES

Measure Distance

Aim of exercise Club selection on the course.

Hit 10 balls on a level fairway or driving range and measure the distance of the longest shot you can hit with each of your clubs. You can also measure the five best shots achieved with each club to get an idea of your average distance at full swing.

The Pivot

Aim of exercise Ensuring correct pivot motion.

Cross your arms on your chest, right hand on left shoulder, left hand on right. Turn your shoulders on a horizontal plane in relation to your spine angle during the full swing.

Scale Test

Aim of exercise Checking your weight distribution at the top of your backswing and follow-through.

When executing a full swing, your weight distribution at the top of the backswing should be approximately 70 percent on the right foot, and on the left foot approximately 90 percent in the finish position.

Weight Transfer

Aim of exercise Understanding the importance of weight transfer during the golf swing.

Correct weight transfer is vital to achieving success in golf. Attempt to emulate the actions in the photographs. You will see that the weight transfer necessary in other sports is similar to that in the golf swing.

BUNKER PLAY

There is far more to read, or assess, in a bunker than on any green in the world. In fact, the most amount of reading that takes place in golf is in the bunker.

Once you are standing in the bunker, first establish what the condition of the sand is. How much of it is there beneath your feet and – if you're not playing on your home course – what type of sand is it?

Then you must read the possible effects that the way your ball is lying will have on the shot. Is the ball on an upslope or a downslope? Is it positioned above your feet or below? If it's on a downslope it will come out low – so what is the height of the front lip? Is it lying close to or under a lip; to the front, back or side; or in a rake mark? Rough soft sand and rake marks impose unfair penalties on the golfer, making it very difficult to recover.

You do not have to change your swing in sand play. Apart from an earlier wrist cock and a slower rhythm, in terms of your usual swing plane it should be the same as that of, say, your medium iron.

Most of the important fundamental changes are made at address. There is no need for a fancy wrist break in the take-away. Do not take the club back outside the line of your feet and shoulders and then pull it down across your body. Once you have set up correctly, go ahead and swing normally – this applies regardless of the lie.

Stance Ensure that the geometry of your stance – the line of your feet and shoulders, in other words – is open to your target line. That means that you should turn your body to your left, with the line of your feet, hips and shoulders pointing well left of your target. When you come to swing, the club will

follow your body alignment as it does with your normal swing using a mid-iron. As the line of your feet, hips and shoulders is open to the target line in the bunker, you are swinging back across the target line and down through it, effectively putting a cut spin (that is, a curve from left to right) on the ball with an open club face. The more open the stance and club face, the greater the spin, and the higher and shorter the shot.

Now you need to build your stance in the bunker to play the standard shot, and it must be one that inhibits any body sway. One of the worst things you can do is stand too narrow, because if your feet are close together there is a tendency to sway. Swaying is bad on any shot, but once you start swaying in a bunker you never hit the same distance behind the ball consistently. So stand with your feet a little wider than in your normal stance. This also stops you from using your legs too much in the swing, which inhibits any weight transfer and makes you use your hands more.

With the ball positioned just inside your left heel, you need to wriggle your feet well into the sand to ensure your stance is firm – you don't want any sinking down or slipping as you swing. You must also brace your right foot, so that its inside edge is lower than its outside one. The build-up of sand outside it will also help to prevent sway.

You should keep your weight more on your left foot than the right, in this case about 60 percent on the left, as this will encourage you to cock your wrists earlier than with your normal swing. You have to take the club back steeply enough to clear the sand. Finally, with your body well braced but not locked stiff, you hover the head of your opened sand wedge above the sand about 1.5in (4cm) behind the ball. This is the point where the club will enter the sand to slide through and emerge some 2in (5cm) beyond the ball, and you should focus your attention on the sand rather than on the ball itself. As you would with a putt, check the area on the green you are aiming for and then look back at that point in the sand. You are now set up for a good shot.

You are going to make a long, smooth, slow swing, differing from your normal one only in that it is slower and has an earlier wrist cock. It is also made with the hands and arms, with no body coil or weight transfer.

Left (top to bottom) Gary Player loses his balance after playing a superb bunker shot on his knees during the 1994 British Seniors Open at Royal Lytham and St Annes.

Backswing From the start of the take-away, as you swing the club back along the line of your feet and shoulders, cock your wrists. The reason is that an early wrist cock is a bit like an elastic band. When you stretch it, it snaps back automatically and with speed. If you go back stiff-wristed, you'll never achieve any speed through the ball.

When the club shaft is parallel to the ground and the line of your feet, and your hands have moved to a position opposite your right thigh, the back of the left hand is pointing forward – not up to the sky, or down to the ground. By the time the arms are horizontal, the club shaft is pointing vertically upward, or a little beyond it. This is a full, early wrist cock.

Swing slowly to avoid hitting down on the ball at a steep angle. If you do that on a fairway and the ground is hard, the club will bounce and you will top the ball (hit the ball above its centre causing it to hop along the ground). In a bunker the opposite happens. Since the sand is soft, if you come down at the ball fast and at a steep angle, you dig deep, compress the sand and stay in the bunker.

In terms of how far back you should swing, you need a long, full swing on all but very short shots. This will give you more time to gauge distance and gain that feel, but guard against decelerating the club as you skim it through the sand.

Downswing The best way to describe the downswing is to think of 'striking a match', which implies a firm, crisp action. If you try to strike a match too hard, its head breaks off. If you decelerate the action and dab at the side of the box, the match doesn't light.

When golfers don't 'strike the match' on the downswing, they decelerate. Their wrists roll over, the club face closes and they dig deep into the sand. By swinging crisply through the sand, you will not have to think about releasing your wrists through impact as this will be automatic.

Follow-through Similarly, a full follow-through makes sure you don't decelerate or leave the club in the sand. On a standard 11yd (10m) shot from a good lie, your hands should end up about chest-high.

There is nothing like practice to build confidence, which is the key to good sand play. The fundamentals reviewed above can be applied to every bunker shot with just a few alterations.

Following pages Early morning light catches golf balls lying on the grass at the Blue Canyon Golf Club in Thailand.

WORKING THE BALL
Backspin

Without backspin, a golf ball would not fly at all. A ball without dimples would fly only a very short distance before dipping sharply back to earth. It is the combination of backspin and the design and depth of the dimple pattern on a ball that allows it to climb, travel the required distance and land again.

The greater the loft on a club, generally the greater the amount of backspin. And when a ball has more backspin, it tends to smother the effects of sidespin on the ball. This is undoubtedly why the average golfer who tends to slice his drives has more control over an 8- or 9-iron.

A lot of golfers try to impart backspin on the ball by chopping down on it extra hard or punching it. This is not the solution! The only way to ensure maximum backspin is by hitting the ball cleanly with the club face square at impact. Achieving this depends on various factors, not least a correct grip and swing plane.

Sidespin is caused by the club face not being square at impact. If the club is open, in other words the heel leads the toe, slice spin will be the result, and the ball will travel from the left to the right. If the club face is closed, with the toe ahead of the heel, hook spin will be imparted on the ball, causing it to travel from right to left.

There are advantages to both types – backspin and sidespin – and a good golfer is able to impart his or her choice of spin on the ball at will.

Hitting a draw

To hit a draw (a controlled right-to-left shot), the golfer has to approach the shot quite differently.

The grip A 'stronger' grip is required. This does not mean that you have to grip the club so tightly that your knuckles turn white. To strengthen the grip means to rotate the hands to the right on the shaft, so that the Vs formed between the thumb and forefinger point to the right of your right shoulder. You should be able to see three knuckles of your left hand when you look down at your hands.

Alignment Your stance should be 'shut', meaning that your shoulders, hips and feet should be aiming slightly right of the target.

In-to-out swing Instead of swinging the club exactly along the line of the target, the club should be swung in-to-out, i.e. from inside the target line before impact to outside the imaginary line after impact.

Closed club face The club face should be closed at impact, which imparts hook spin on the ball.

Hitting a fade
As a fade (a controlled left-to-right shot) is the exact opposite of the draw, it follows that you should carry out the opposite action.

The grip A 'weaker' grip is required. The converse of a 'strong' grip, a weak grip is achieved by rotating the hands to the left on the shaft of the club. You will probably only be able to see one knuckle of your left hand on the shaft.

Alignment An open stance is required – shoulders, hips and feet aiming to the left of the target.

Out-to-in swing The club approaches the ball from outside the line, continuing inside the line after impact.

Open club face At impact the club face is open, with the heel leading the toe, which will result in slice spin.

Right *Gary Player has won golf tournaments in five decades, from the 1950s through to the 1990s. It is not impossible for him to become the first person to win in six decades.*

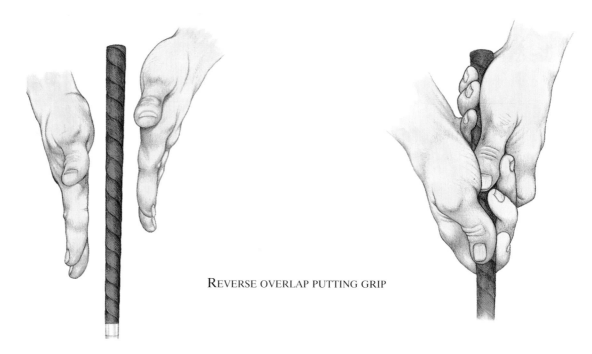

REVERSE OVERLAP PUTTING GRIP

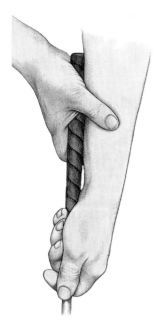

LANGER GRIP

PUTTING

"Putting is more or less half of the game of golf, so if you want to win tournaments, you should follow the pro's proverb: 'We'll drive for show but putt for dough.' Spend at least a third of your practice time improving your putting."

— *Gary Player*

Putting is the art of hitting the ball along the surface of the green so it rolls into the hole. The swing concept of the putt is to swing the hands and therefore the club head back and then towards the hole, directly along the target line. The ball should be hit keeping the club face square (at 90 degrees) to the target line and the hole. When practising putting, the finest aid to check all of the above is to create a 'club lane' (*see* illustration opposite) along the target line towards the hole. Two clubs are placed on either side of your ball about 12in (30cm) apart, parallel to the target line. A third club is placed square to the club lane opposite your ball.

The putting grip

The grip to use when putting is more a personal preference, but one of the important aspects of any putting grip is that both palms face each other with the same amount of pressure being exerted by each hand. The reverse overlap grip is probably the most commonly used putting grip in the world today, by professionals and amateurs alike. It is a simple adap-

tation of the Vardon, or standard overlapping grip, described on page 68. The only difference is that instead of the little finger of the right hand overlapping the forefinger of the left hand, the forefinger of the left hand overlaps the fingers of the right hand. This helps to keep the left hand, arm and shoulder moving correctly through the ball, and eliminates any wrist action in the putting stroke.

The Langer grip

The 'yips' is an affliction – a result of nerves – which affects golfers, causing them to jerk and twitch, leading to a stabbing, uncontrollable putting action. The yips can affect your average club golfer and it can also ruin the career of a seasoned pro. Top German golfer Bernhard Langer found himself with a severe case of the putting yips in the 1980s which led him to experiment with different grips and putters in what proved to be a successful attempt to beat the problem.

In the process he devised what is now known as the Langer grip: the left hand grips the putter handle just above where the grip meets the shaft, with the left forearm kept straight, parallel to the shaft and resting against the top of the club handle. The right hand grasps both the upper part of the putter grip and the left forearm, 'locking' the putter onto the left arm firmly to avoid movement during the stroke. This grip effectively eliminates all wrist action when putting.

GARY PLAYER'S PUTTING PRACTICE

As with any golf shot, it is vital to have a good grip. There are more variations of the grip for putting than for other shots, but they all have the same fundamentals. For the right-handed golfer, the back of the left hand and the right palm should both face the target.

Getting the right grip Hold the putter with the left hand, the left thumb on the flat part of the putter and pointing directly down the shaft. The club is primarily held with the last three fingers of the left hand. Now place the right hand on the grip so that the heel of the hand covers the left thumb. The little finger lies on top of the left, middle and index fingers and the right thumb lies on the flat part of the grip, also pointing down the shaft.

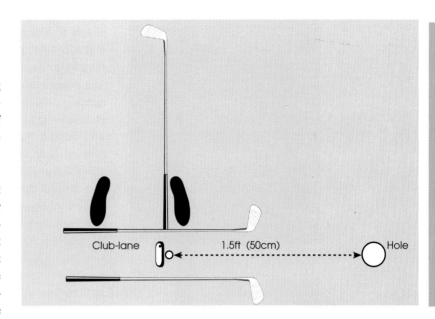

CREATING A CLUB-LANE

Ball position The ball should be placed in line with, or just inside, the left foot.

Stance The feet are placed hip-width apart. The feet, elbows and shoulders should all be aligned parallel to the target line and the player's eyes should be directly over the ball. (Try the ball drop test: a ball dropped from a position between the eyes should land on the ball being addressed.) Both knees should be slightly bent as should both elbows.

Swing The swing concept is that you swing the club along a straight line to the hole with your arms, keeping wrists firm. Your head should be kept perfectly still throughout the swing, and the wrists should not be cocked at all throughout the putt.

On the backswing, keep the club head low to the ground. Ensure that there is always acceleration through the ball on the downswing, no matter how short the putt. After completing the swing, the left wrist should still be in line with the back of the left hand and forearm, and the club face should still be square to the hole.

Use the club lane to set up correctly.

Pendulum putting stroke The pendulum putting style is the most successful and most widely used in the world of tournament golf. The method gets its name from the backwards and forwards movement of a clock pendulum, and when practised correctly, there is very little that can go wrong. The triangle formed by the shoulders and the arms pivots in one piece from a point round about the base of the neck. The hands play no active part at all, merely forming a link between the arms and the putter. As soon as the wrists hinge, allowing the hands to play an active part in the stroke, it is almost impossible to make the action repeat time after time, especially when playing under pressure.

GARY PLAYER'S PUTTING PRACTICE AND GAMES
Backwards and Forwards

Aim of the exercise Getting the ball into the hole from increasing distances.

Practise using the club lane, but have a little competition with yourself. First putt from approximately 20in (50cm) from the hole. If you sink the putt, keep moving the ball 12in (30cm) backwards each time until you miss sinking the putt. If you at first miss, move the ball 12in (30cm) forward again until you sink that putt. Once you have achieved some measure of success, do the same exercise again, but this time without the club lane.

Club Face to the Hole

Aim of exercise Swinging along the target line, accelerating during the forward swing.

Place the ball 12in (30cm) from the hole. Ensure that after hitting it, the club face ends up squarely over the hole.

Putter Grip against Left Inside of Forearm

Aim of exercise Keeping a firm left wrist during the whole swing.

Using a tennis wristband or something similar, anchor the putter grip against the inside of your left forearm and then practise sinking the putt from various distances.

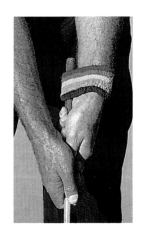

Hit the Ball with Eyes Closed

Aim of exercise Concentrating on correct swing movement.

Close your eyes after addressing the ball and swing the club back and then towards the target. Listen for the sound of the ball dropping into the hole.

Ladder Game

Aim of exercise Getting the feel of hitting putts of different distances. Place six to eight tees about 12in (30cm) apart in a straight line on the green. Stand about 2yd (2m) from the first tee and hit a series of balls at each tee in sequence, starting with the first one.

Long Putts

Aim of exercise Getting the ball as close to the hole as possible.

When faced with a long putt, try to roll the ball into an imaginary circle 3ft (1m) in diameter around the hole. By widening the target you will be more relaxed for your stroke.

Balls in a Circle Around the Hole

Aim of exercise Sinking the ball from different angles.

Place eight balls in a circle around the hole, about 20in (50cm) from the hole. Stroke them into the hole one after the other. Once each ball has been successfully holed, widen the circle by increasing the distance from the balls to the hole. This exercise is best done on a slightly undulating green so that all types of putts are incorporated.

Ball Curve

Aim of exercise Getting the right combination of distance and direction for curving putts.

Visualize the line of the curving putt. Place 8 to 10 balls about 12in (30cm) apart along this line. Putt the ball nearest the hole first and then each successive ball, aiming over the spot where the previous ball was and giving it the speed that will make it roll into the hole. The club head must still move along a straight line, but to the spot where the previous ball lay, and not directly to the hole.

Most often on a golf course, the line from your ball to the hole will not be a straight one. This is what the art of putting is all about. You have to imagine the curve of the ball depending on the slope and the grain of the grass. However, every putt must be played like a straight putt. So, once you have judged the curve of your putt, choose an imaginary hole above the actual hole and execute a straight putt to your imaginary hole, letting the green take the ball to the actual hole.

A Putter Length Back

Aim of exercise Practising a combination of both long and short putts.
Place a ball approximately five club-lengths from the hole. Attempt to putt the ball into the hole. If you don't sink the putt, move the ball a full putter length nearer to the hole and attempt to hole out again. Repeat until the ball is successfully holed.

STRETCH EXERCISES

Flexibility is as important as strength when it comes to swinging a golf club and hitting a golf ball. Remember that club head speed comes from a full, unrestricted swing, which can only be achieved by a full body turn. The exercises that follow will help maintain the ability to do this.

Neck Stretch

Place one hand behind the head and stretch the other down next to the body. Slowly pull the head to the side and push down with the extended arm. Hold for 6–12 seconds. Repeat. Change positions.

Bent-over Shoulder Stretch

Sit on a chair and stretch arms behind your back, interlocking your fingers. Bend over and pull arms slowly up and over your back.

Shoulder Stretch
Variation 1

With legs comfortably apart, place hands on the floor behind you (fingers pointing forwards). Slowly push forward with the knees so that the necessary stretch can be felt on the shoulder muscle group. NB: Do not remain in this position for too long.

Variation 2

With legs comfortably apart, place hands on the floor (fingers pointing backwards). Repeat the same actions as for Variation 1.

Triceps Pull/Shoulder Stretch

Stand in an upright position. Hold a club in both hands behind the back. Keep one arm extended (with the hand placed on the club head) and flex the other arm up behind the head, holding onto the grip of the club. Push down with the extended arm and feel the triceps stretch with the upper flexed arm. Reverse the arm after holding a static stretch for at least 8 seconds.

Forearm/Wrist Stretch

Start on all fours (knees and hands), placing hands on the floor with fingers pointing towards the knees. Keep palms flat and lean gently back to stretch the front forearms. Hold the stretch for 8–12 seconds.

Spinal Twist (Seated)

Sit on a chair and point both feet straight ahead. Slowly turn the upper body around and place both hands at waist-height on the chair rest. Hold for 8–12 seconds. Release the grip and turn slowly back to a normal sitting position. Repeat the same action to the opposite side.

Chest, Shoulder and Back Stretch

Variation 1

Stretch both hands behind the back, interlocking fingers with palms facing upward and elbows facing inwards.

Variation 2

Repeat the same procedure as for Variation 1 but with palms facing downwards and elbows facing outwards.
Note: Both Variations 1 and 2 can be enhanced by lifting both arms upward for additional stretch. These exercises also improve posture.

'Lat'/Shoulder Stretch

Crouch on the knees a comfortable distance from a chair. Place both hands on the seat of the chair (arms extended). Keep the head between the arms. Push down from the shoulders and feel the 'lats' (latissimus dorsi) stretching on the downward movement.

Standing Hamstring Stretch

With one leg bent, extend the other leg and place it on a chair seat, holding onto the extended leg for support. Lean forward from the hips, extending your back. Inhale on the way down and exhale when reaching your own personal maximum range. Inhale to support the back. Hold for 8–10 seconds. Straighten up and repeat. NB: Do not force head down.

Seated Hamstring Stretch

Keep one leg extended and one leg bent. Place hands on the extended leg and inhale as you bend down. Exhale when reaching your own personal maximum range.
NB: Do not force the head down.

Standing Quadriceps Stretch

With one hand, hold onto a chair or any other device for balance. With the other hand, pull the heel of one foot up to the buttocks and feel the quadriceps stretch. Bend the other leg slightly to reduce the stress of the lower back.

Quadriceps Stretch (Lying)

Lie down face forward and place forehead onto the left arm. Bend knees and take hold of the right forefoot with the right hand. Pull the heel towards the buttocks with a slow, controlled action and hold for a count of 8–12 seconds. Change to the other side and repeat the same action. NB: Keep the head down.

Hip Flexor Stretch
Variation 1

This improvised lunge is a preparatory step for an advanced lunge. Place one foot on the seat of a chair or bench. Both feet must remain aligned with one another. Keep a straight back and place both hands on the raised knee for support.

Variation 2

This advanced stretch is done as follows:
Keep the rear leg in an extension with the back and neck. Rest the trunk on the bent leg (at a 90-degree angle) and place the hands on either side on the floor. Change legs and repeat the action.

Seated Groin Stretch

Sit down on the ground, with knees bent and feet in front of you, soles facing each other. Hold onto the feet with the hands and extend elbows out wide. Start in an upright position, inhale, then slowly bend down to the feet. Exhale and relax. Hold for between 8–15 seconds, inhale and return to the starting position. Exhale.

Spinal Column Stress Release Exercises/'Cat Stretch'

Go down on all fours. Keep the back straight as an extension of the vertebral column, and inhale. Pull the head in, contract the abdominals and round the back as functionally as possible, and exhale. Hold for between 8–12 seconds and return to the starting position.

Seated Cross-leg Back Stretch

In a seated position, cross right leg over the extended left leg. With a straight back, inhale, turn with the trunk, place your right arm on the floor to your left side and move the other arm straight back on the floor behind. Exhale and relax in that position. Hold for 8–10 seconds. Inhale, turn forward slowly with the trunk, and exhale. Change leg and arm positions and repeat the exercise.

Single Knee-tuck

Lie on your back. Inhale and with your hands pull the knee onto the chest. Bring the head up to meet the knee and exhale. Hold for 8 seconds, then return to the starting position and change legs.

Double Knee-tuck
Variation 1
Go through the same procedures as for single knee-tuck, but instead wrap the arms around the top of both knees and pull onto the chest.

Variation 2
Same procedures as above, but now cross the arms in the crook of the bent knees. Hold onto the elbows and pull onto the chest.

Double Knee-bent Rotations
Lie back. Place arms flat on the floor, bend legs and bring knees up to the chest. Inhale and turn both legs (bent knees) to one side until they make contact with the floor. Exhale and relax. Hold for 8 seconds. Inhale, pull knees up, return to centre, exhale and relax. Repeat the same procedure to the other side.
NB: Do not do this movement with straight legs and keep the knees close to the chest.

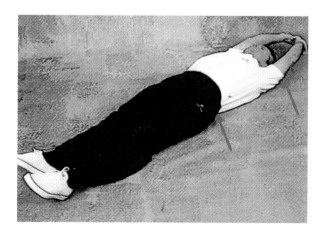

Elongation Stretch
Lie back, extend the arms behind the head and straighten out the legs. Attempt to reach as far as is comfortable, with arms and legs stretching in opposite directions. Hold for 10 seconds and relax.

E X E R C I S E S

ADDITIONAL STRENGTHENING EXERCISES

The following strengthening exercises are designed to strengthen and tone the muscles that are used in the golf swing. As with any type of exercise, start slowly and stop immediately should you feel undue pain or discomfort.

Book Lifts

Hold a fairly large book between the palms. Extend the arms forward and twist the wrists up and back down again, with the book firmly in place. For variation, increase the book size.

Forearm Rotation

Begin as for above, but after extending the arms, rotate the forearms to the left and then to the right.

Wrist Rotation

Hold a heavy club in one hand. Lift the club head off the ground and move the club head in small circles. Increase the circles until you feel the strain in the wrist and forearm.

Left Forearm Rotation

Hold a club in the left hand. Lift up straight left arm in front of you to shoulder-height, and cock the wrist so that the thumb and club shaft are pointing up. Turn the left thumb to the right side (pronation), then back and to the left (supination). The wrist should stay in line with the back of the hand and forearm. For variation, increase the repetitions.

Swing a Heavy Club

Swing a heavy club as for a right-handed golfer and then as for a left-handed golfer, to develop your muscles on both sides.

Left Arm Swing

Grip a heavy club with the left hand only. Imitate your golf swing by using your left arm.

Squeezing a Tennis Ball

Hold a tennis ball in the palm of the hand and squeeze it repeatedly with the fingers. Increase the compression of the tennis ball.

Winding up a Weight

Tie a weighted object (e.g. a bucket of stones) to the centre of a short length of pole, using a piece of string approximately 3ft (1m) long. Holding the pole parallel to the ground, stretch the arms forward and wind the string around the pole by twisting it in your hands until the weight touches the pole. For variation, increase the rolling speed of the weight.

Club Lifts

Hold a heavy club (keep the club cover on) in one hand in the normal address position. Lift the club until the club head is pointing towards the sky. Repeat until your arm becomes tired. Continue afterwards with the other arm.

CHAPTER SIX

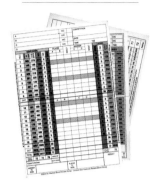

STRATEGY AND COMPETITIVE PLAY

STRATEGY

You can swing a club but can you read a hole? Each hole requires a different strategy. Before playing the first shot from the tee, the golfer should plan how to play the hole.

All golf courses are full of problems and hazards and how the golfer – novice or professional – copes with them is crucial for consistent good scoring. It is essential always to remember to play within one's ability – not everyone has the skills to get around every situation that presents itself on the course, no matter how good one's fantasies are.

Knowing your limits with your clubs is also essential. In a pressure situation it's always best to use the club in the bag that you are most confident with. Everyone has a favourite, or 'faithful', club that can be hauled out to play a safe shot when it's required.

Golfers are always advised to play 'percentage golf', that is, playing the safer option and avoiding risks. Weigh up each shot on its merits, deciding on the possibilities of success or failure, the possible results thereof, and then making a decision considering the risks.

For just about every situation that a golfer faces, there is a safer, more conservative route to take and a player who has good course-management skills

Previous pages The trophy awarded to the winner of the world's oldest and most prestigious amateur tournament, the British Amateur, which was first held in 1885.

In competitive play, it is vital to know how to score correctly.

will know just when to play safe and when to attack. It is vital to a good round to forgive yourself for a poor shot, and to approach the following shot with the same positive attitude you had in setting out on the first tee shot of the day.

Once in trouble – and every golfer will get into trouble during a round – it is best to choose the safe way out, even if that means playing sideways to get

your golfing life, it is fairly pointless trying to emulate him.

What every average golfer can learn from the professionals is their patience and ability to remain focused on the task at hand. They seldom rush into a shot before they have considered every option, they know exactly how far they have to go and they know how far they hit each club.

Here are some common situations that golfers will face on the course and tips on how to deal with them.

ON THE TEE

The tee is the one place where the golfer has the chance to place the ball in the best possible spot from which to approach the hole. Take a few moments to take in as much information about the hole as you can. Look at where the hazards are, look for the danger areas, and above all pick out a target which has the most safety around it.

Try to choose the flattest part of the tee on which to take up your stance – unless, of course, you want to deliberately hit a fade or a draw (*see* pages 90–91); then a slight slope may assist your planned shot. It is advisable to tee the ball on the side closest to the trouble, which usually helps you to play away from it.

Once you have assessed where the hazards are, and assuming that you are playing percentage golf, choose a club that ensures you avoid the hazards, even if you miss-hit the shot. Don't be fooled into thinking that just because you are on the tee of a par four or par five, you must pull out the driver and try to whack it 300yd (270m) down the fairway. Because of a driver's lack of loft and longer shaft, it will certainly hit the ball further, but it is more difficult to control and consistency is more difficult to

the ball back in play. Then put the lapse out of your mind and continue with the round as before.

Choices on the golf course will, of course, vary depending on the level of experience and skill at the golfer's disposal. It's all very well watching a talented professional cutting the corner over the trees of a dogleg, but if you can only hit the ball 220yd (200m) downhill, downwind, on the best day of

"I PLAN TO WIN SO MUCH MONEY THIS YEAR, MY CADDY'S GONNA FINISH IN THE TOP 20 MONEY WINNERS."

— *LEE TREVINO*

achieve. A fairway wood, with it's greater loft, may well be a better option.

Check other factors such as the direction and strength of the wind and also the slope of the fairway. Once you have chosen a club and have a picture of the intended shot, stick with it and commit yourself to doing what you envisaged. If any doubt as to what you are about to do should creep in while you are standing over the ball, back away from the shot and start the planning process again. Indecision is a sure-fire way of getting a poor result.

ON THE FAIRWAY

Having successfully played from the tee onto the fairway, you can start thinking about your next shot as you stroll up the fairway. Be careful not to make all the decisions about the next shot before reach-

Fairways provide the best lies for the ball, allowing for a cleaner hit and more control of the ball.

ing your ball, though – a few yards can make a lot of difference to the view of your next shot. Once at your ball, check your lie, make sure that the ball is lying cleanly and not obstructed by tufts of grass or lying in a divot.

Once you have worked out the required distance of the next shot, check danger areas, hazards and the 'bail-out' area again, just as on the tee. If this partic-

ular shot is an approach shot to the green, check the green's shape and size and the position of the flag. If the flag is tucked close to a water hazard or behind a bunker, weigh up the dangers of aiming directly for the hole. Aim rather at the 'heart' of the green. It's always easier to bag a birdie (*see* page 118) with a longish putt than with a bunker shot. If the green has obvious slopes, always try to land your approach below the hole, leaving yourself with an uphill putt to the hole. Uphill putts can always be struck with more confidence than an attempt to trickle a slippery downhill putt to the hole.

If you are playing your second shot on a long par four or a par five and are not aiming to reach the green, don't necessarily try to hit the ball as close to the green as possible. A full wedge or sand-wedge shot is easier than having to play a finesse three-quarter shot to a tough pin placement.

IN THE ROUGH

So what you were trying to avoid has happened! Don't berate yourself all the way from the tee to your ball for being so stupid – forget the bad swing

Grass between the ball and the club face reduces backspin, so allow for this when playing from the rough.

and concentrate on what you should be doing. Once you've located your ball, assess the severity of the situation. Remember that the longer grass and resultant poor lie is going to affect the contact of the club on the ball, thereby reducing backspin and control.

Bearing in mind that the chances of a poor shot are increased out of the rough, take a more critical look at the dangers facing your shot. If need be, take your 'punishment' and use a lofted iron to play a safe shot back onto the fairway, giving yourself a chance to make up for your error with a good shot from the fairway. That way, the chances are you will only drop one shot rather than risk dropping more by playing another poor shot deeper into trouble.

IN THE TREES

Don't be fooled by the optimists who will tell you that trees are made up of 80 percent air! Wood provides excellent resistance to surlyn and balata alike. If you are an experienced player and are able to play

A trying moment for Ernie Els during the 1994 Masters at Augusta, in Atlanta, Georgia.

high or low shots, you may be able to get out of trouble reasonably easily. Remember, though, that your main aim is to get out of trouble and not land the ball a yard from the hole; so the definition of an excellent shot changes, and you should be happy with getting out of trouble in the general direction of the hole. There's nothing more irritating than watching a golfer playing a miraculous escape shot from a forest, only to watch him bend his club around the nearest elm because he missed an easy putt.

IN A FAIRWAY BUNKER

A fairway bunker need not be a disaster to a player's fortunes on a hole. Depending on the lie and the height of the lip in front of the ball, a very successful

Confidence, and a full follow-through, are keys to a successful shot from a fairway bunker.

shot can be executed. Fairway bunkers will usually be less severe than their counterparts around the green, and a clean shot will often end in a very satisfactory result. Aim to hit the ball cleanly, taking as little sand as possible. Take one more club than normal for the distance to the green and take a controlled, smooth swing at the ball. When taking your stance, make sure that your feet are firmly planted in the sand, and try to restrict body movement as much as possible.

If the ball is plugged, or the front of the bunker is particularly high, the percentage shot is to get the ball back on the fairway and to play from there.

Only the very brave should try playing out of water.

ROUTINES

Develop a preshot routine that can be used for every shot you play. A routine helps to focus the mind on the 30 seconds or so that you need to concentrate intensely on making a good swing. A player cannot be expected to concentrate on nothing else but his swing for the full four hours that it takes to play 18 holes, so a preshot routine helps to focus on the job at hand. A typical routine would contain the following:

1. Once the club has been chosen, take one or two practice swings, concentrating on smoothness and rhythm.

2. Stand behind the ball and follow the intended flight path from the ball to the target.

3. Pick a spot on the ground about 3ft (1m) in front of the ball, directly on the line to the target.

4. Take up your stance parallel to this imaginary line. You now know that you are aiming correctly, which is often half the battle in hitting the ball to the target. Try to have only one or two key swing thoughts when you are actually playing the shot. Trying to think about too many things at once is likely to be confusing. Trust that your body knows what to do, and play the shot.

WATER HAZARDS

It is seldom possible to play out of a water hazard, so extra care should be taken when faced with water on a hole. The higher handicapper should make a conscious effort to play away from it or short of it to the safer area of the hole, and the better player, too, should approach the situation with more caution. Make sure that you know the difference between a water hazard and a lateral water hazard, and know the options available to you if you do land up in the 'drink'.

AROUND THE GREEN

Without exception, every great golfer, no matter how far or well he can hit the ball, will have an excellent short game. This is where shots are saved and good rounds become great rounds. A golfer has to accept that he is going to miss the green with his approach shot

Swede Helen Alfredsson pitches towards the hole.

When on the fringe, a low running chip shot is often best to get close to the hole.

more than once in a round. In order to save par, he must be able to get 'up and down' in two shots as often as possible.

Around the green there are numerous short shots that present themselves, from a high, soft-landing lob shot to a low running chip shot (a short, lofted shot). Always check how much green you have to

The green is the only place where the ball can be marked, picked up and cleaned.

work with and then choose the shot over which you have most control. Don't be afraid to use your putter from off the green as a percentage shot – you'll often have more control over the putter and therefore a greater chance of putting closer to the hole. The chip shot is the next easiest, but you have to have enough green between yourself and the pin because the ball will tend to roll a long way.

The toughest of the short shots around the green is the high lob to a tight pin position or over a greenside bunker. Here it is critical to be committed to the shot, as any indecision is likely to end in a thin shot (the ball is not hit cleanly) that could endanger the ankles of your playing partners on the other side of the green!

If you are unsure of your chances of successfully completing the shot, aim at the greater part of the green, away from the flag. At least from here you have the chance of sinking a longer putt, rather than having to play another chip shot from off the green or, worse still, a bunker shot that should not have been necessary.

ON THE GREEN

The Rules of Golf allow for the marking of the ball with a pen to identify it on the course, and the cleaning of the ball on the green. Get into the habit of doing this each time before you putt, as a clean ball will roll better. It also forces you to slow down a bit, giving you time to assess what needs to be done to get the ball in the hole. Be firm with your putts and always aim to stop the ball a few centimetres past the hole – as clichéd as 'never up, never in' sounds, it is nonetheless true.

When faced with a tricky turning putt, pick a spot to the side of the hole to aim at, and then treat the putt as a dead straight one. Concentrate on taking a smooth stroke at the ball – don't try to guide it into the hole because that's when you tend to push or pull your putts.

COMPETITIVE PLAY

Essentially, the aim of golf is to complete nine or 18 holes in as few shots as possible, the person hitting the fewest being adjudged the winner. Largely this is true of professional golf tournaments, where everyone plays the course 'off scratch' – in other words, there is no use of handicaps to decide the winner. The beauty of golf is that with the help of a handicap, any player – no matter his experience or ability – can take on another player, again of any skill, and have an extremely competitive game.

Handicap

A handicap in golf does not necessarily refer to the shortcomings of the golfer! It is a figure, usually between zero and 36, attributed to a player that allows him or her to play on an equal basis against any other golfer. Handicaps are calculated by working out the difference between a player's total score over 18 holes and comparing it to par or course rating (*see* panel opposite). A handicap committee at a club then decides, according to a series of scores handed in by the player and a chosen formula, what his handicap should be. Usually the handicap is calculated as 80 percent of the difference between the total score and the course rating, e.g. if you hand in scores of 98, 97, 93, 96, 91 and 93, and your home course has a par of 72 and a course rating of 71, your handicap could be calculated as being 19.

$$95 \text{ (average of 6 scores)} - 71 = 24$$
$$\times 80\% = 19$$

Unfortunately, for handicapping purposes, scoring becomes a little more complicated. Unlike in a

SCORING FOR HANDICAP PURPOSES

To fill in your score after a hole, find out the stroke index for that hole. The stroke index is displayed on all scorecards and gives a rating of difficulty for each hole. If the stroke index is less than your handicap, you get a shot (i.e. one stroke) on that hole: your net score is then one less than your gross score on that hole. If the stroke index is more than your handicap, your net score is the same as your gross score.

For handicapping purposes, you may not score more than a net bogey (see page 118) on any hole. For example, if you score a seven on a par four on which you get a shot, you have to write down a six with a circle around it. If, however, you score a seven on a par four on which you do not get a shot, you have to write down a five with a circle around it.

This system has been devised in order to restrict radical changes in handicaps, often favoured by 'the ringer', who contrives to manufacture his or her handicap with the sole purpose of winning club competitions.

strokeplay or medal competition, where every shot played counts, for handicapping purposes this would be unsuitable. If a single-figure golfer had a nightmare score on one hole, e.g. a 12 on a par three (it's been known to happen to the best), it would be unthinkable to increase his handicap by five or six shots just because of one hole. For this reason, handicapping committees allow a player to score a maximum of net one over on each hole.

What does this mean? On every course each hole is rated from 1 to 18 according to the perceived difficulty – the most difficult being rated 1 and the easiest, 18. This is the stroke index.

An understanding of hole ratings is important when it comes to playing a myriad club competitions, and when it comes to working out the net score on each hole. If a player has a handicap of 18, it's quite simple: he just subtracts one shot from his score on each hole on the course. Once a player has a handicap of less than 18, one shot is subtracted only on holes on which the player gets a shot (see panel above). Therefore if you improve your game substantially and you achieve a handicap of 12, you can only subtract one shot on holes that have a stroke index of 1 to 12.

TYPES OF COMPETITIONS
STROKEPLAY, OR MEDAL

Referred to earlier, this is the basis from which the game of golf has evolved. Simply explained, this competition requires the golfer to go out, tee off, and then count every shot that he plays until he has holed out on every hole on the 18-hole course. Failure to complete any hole will result in disqualification. The golfer adds up the total number of shots, compares it with his or her fellow competitors, and the golfer with the lowest total wins.

Handicaps are used to determine the net winner. The golfer's handicap is deducted from his or her gross total to calculate the net total, and is then compared with the net total of fellow competitors. The person who has the lowest net total is declared the winner.

Naturally, the chances are high that more than one player will have the same lowest total, with the result that, depending on the competition, the tournament officials will either require that a 'sudden death' is played (the first player to win another designated hole wins the match) or they will add the scores on alternate holes to the tied scores.

The most famous of the strokeplay championships are without doubt the four so-called Majors. These are the ultimate tournaments that every professional golfer sets his sights on winning, thereby gaining worldwide fame and untold fortune.

The oldest of the four is the British Open, or the Open Championship, as it is referred to by the purists, dating back to 1860. The youngest of the four is the US Masters dating back to 1934.

COURSE AND HOLE RATINGS

Even though a course's par may be 72, it will not necessarily have a rating of the same. A standard system has been devised so that courses can be compared to one another fairly. This is to ensure that a golfer's handicap reflects his overall golfing ability rather than simply how well he plays a particular course.

Factors that are considered include: the overall length, the altitude at which the course is situated, the size of fairway target areas, difficulties near target areas, size and location of green, and ground slopes.

Individual holes are also rated using the above factors, and are then listed from 1 to 18 – 1 being the most difficult and 18 the easiest. This is called the stroke index and is important when assessing whether a player receives a shot on a hole according to his handicap.

MAJOR CHAMPIONSHIPS

Nick Faldo hands a green jacket to Tiger Woods, who won the Masters in 1997.

THE MASTERS TOURNAMENT

Played annually in April, the Masters is the only Major played at the same course each year – the famed Augusta National in Atlanta, Georgia, USA. What once was a friendly invitation event for American Bobby Jones and his buddies has become golf's most spectacular extravaganza. Jones's Invitational Tournament had already been branded the Masters by 1938, but during the 1940s, like most other things during World War II, golf had to take a back seat. The Masters resumed in 1946, in which year Herman Keiser defeated Ben Hogan by one shot. Hogan and Sam Snead dominated in the 1950s, winning four Masters between them, and then in 1961 Gary Player became the first overseas champion. The triumvirate of Jack Nicklaus, Gary Player and Tom Watson dominated in the 1960s and 1970s, with Player winning for the last time in 1978.

The 1980s saw more invitations going to the European-based players, and Severiano Ballesteros, Bernhard Langer, Sandy Lyle and Nick Faldo brought the American dominance of the tournament to an abrupt halt. Nevertheless, this period still saw the 46-year-old Golden Bear, Jack Nicklaus, return to the winner's rostrum to collect the coveted green jacket.

The 1990s have been overshadowed by the arrival of Tiger Woods at Augusta, who in his first appearance there as a professional smashed just about every existing record, winning by an incredible 12 shots in 1997.

THE US OPEN CHAMPIONSHIP

The first US Open was staged in 1895 with 10 professionals in the field and one amateur. An Englishman, Horace Rawlins, triumphed at the Newport Golf Club nine-hole course with rounds of 91 and 82, collecting £150 for his troubles.

In 1898, the first time the event was played over 72 holes, Fred Herd – born in St Andrews, Scotland – won with a score of 328. He carried his own bag which contained just seven clubs that he had made himself.

Gary Player won the US Open only once, in 1965 at Bellerive Country Club in St Louis, Missouri, after an 18-hole play-off with Australian Kel Nagle.

Since its humble beginnings, the US Open has become America's greatest test of strokeplay golf with the tournament always played on the longest, tightest layouts possible. The rough at the chosen courses is allowed to grow thick and creep into the fairways, ensuring that only the professional with the very best all-round game emerges as the victor on the Sunday of the tournament. Winning scores close to par are not uncommon.

Mark O'Meara wins the Claret Jug in 1998.

THE BRITISH OPEN

First played in 1860, the first 12 Opens were held at Prestwick before the event moved to another links course, St Andrews. A total of 14 venues, all links courses, have been used since 1860, although only eight of these are on today's official roster. After World War I the running of the Open was passed from the hands of the individual clubs to the R&A, who still run it today. During the 1950s, American dominance declined as fewer players made the long trip to Britain, and the Open began to lose its prestige as the premier tournament in the world. Arnold Palmer changed that with two victories in the early 1960s, and Americans started returning in their droves.

Turnberry in 1977 was the scene of one of the most memorable Opens when Americans Tom Watson and Jack Nicklaus matched each other stroke for stroke, round for round over the first three rounds. Watson finished the final round with back-to-back birdies to win his second of five Opens by a single shot from Nicklaus.

Nick Price kisses the Wanamaker Trophy in the US PGA in 1994.

THE US PGA CHAMPIONSHIP

Originally played as a matchplay event, the PGA changed to strokeplay in 1958.

Traditionally the US PGA is played in August each year, and is thus the final of the four Majors. Although it tends to receive less media attention than the others, its past champions have nonetheless been some of the greatest names in golf.

American John Daly smashed his way into the big time when Zimbabwean Nick Price pulled out of the 1991 PGA at Crooked Stick at the last moment. Using Price's caddie, Squeaky, the big-hitting Daly powered his way to victory over an astonished field of pros. Fittingly, Price returned the following year to Bellerive in St Louis, Missouri, to win his first Major at the age of 35. In 1994 he repeated that triumph, having won the British Open in the same year, thus earning the top spot in the world rankings. Nick Price is the only two-time champion of the US PGA Championship in the last 15 years.

OTHER MAJOR MATCHPLAY AND TEAM EVENTS

Seve Ballesteros holds the Ryder Cup in 1997.

RYDER CUP

This is possibly the most famous of all the team events and a competition in which every professional from the USA and Europe would dearly love to play. Twelve players make up each team and the three-day match consists of eight foursomes, eight four-balls (four golfers, two a side, each with his own ball) and 12 singles. It was first played in 1927 between the USA and Great Britain and Ireland, but later Great Britain and Ireland were allowed to enlist players from the rest of Europe. Played every two years, 1997 saw the event played on the European continent for the first time.

Els and Westner, 1996.

WORLD CUP

Played every two years in different parts of the world, the World Cup is contested by teams of two from 32 countries who play four rounds of aggregate strokeplay. The winning country is that with the lowest aggregate total for all four rounds.

US team winners celebrate at St Andrews in 1996.

ALFRED DUNHILL CUP

Also a team event except the teams consist of three players from each country, and countries play medal matchplay in a knock-out format. It is played at St Andrews every year, late in the European summer, and is notorious for its bitterly cold weather.

Peter Thomson, 1998.

SOLHEIM CUP

This match, the women's equivalent of the Ryder Cup, was only very recently established (1990).

US team winners, 1998.

WALKER CUP

The premier amateur team match in the world, The Walker Cup is played between teams from the USA and Great Britain and Ireland every two years. The two-day match consists of eight foursomes and 16 singles matches.

PRESIDENTS CUP

Introduced in 1994 as a 'Ryder Cup-type' event between the USA and the rest of the world excluding Europe, the Presidents Cup has given such big-names as South African Ernie Els, Australian Greg Norman and Zimbabwean Nick Price an opportunity to play major professional team events.

Winning Swedish team, 1992.

CURTIS CUP

This is the amateur women's equivalent of the Walker Cup.

Walker Cup.

MATCHPLAY

In matchplay the game is played by number of holes won or lost (one player against another or teams of two playing against each other); a hole is won by the side that holes its ball in the fewest strokes. In a match where handicaps are taken into account, the lower net score wins the hole. The score is kept in so many 'holes up' or 'holes down', and so many 'to play'. If a side is 'dormie', there are as many holes to play as the side is holes up. A match is won when a side is ahead by a greater number of holes than are remaining to be played.

In matchplay a golfer is allowed to concede a hole or even a match at any time prior to the conclusion of the hole or the match. Generally in matchplay, the penalty imposed on a player who breaches a rule is loss of that hole on which the infringement occurs. Matchplay is one of numerous competitions where the golfer not only plays against the course and himself, but also against his opponent. Mental pressure can thus be cleverly applied to the opponent.

The World Matchplay Championship played at Wentworth in England is possibly the most important matchplay event in professional golf. As matchplay is seldom engaged in by professionals in tournament play, the organizers have to rely on inviting most of the participants as there is no sure way of ranking the professionals through the year. They try to get at least one representative from each major golf tour from around the world in order to maintain the international flavour of the event.

OTHER COMPETITIONS

Golf would be a fairly uninteresting game if everybody only played strokeplay and matchplay all the time. Over the years, many other competitions have been devised both for variety and also simply for pure fun. Below are the common and some not-so-common competitions that the average golfer might find himself playing in a social game, club day or sponsored golf day.

Singles The most common form of two-ball golf. One player competes directly against another during matchplay. The higher handicap player generally receives three-quarters of the difference between the handicaps.

Foursomes Two players form a side and hit alternate shots with the same ball; partners alternate the tee shot on each hole. The handicap allowance is as above, although obviously on a team basis this time.

Greensomes Two players form a side and both drive from the same tee. They then select the best drive and proceed as foursomes from that point, i.e. playing alternate shots until the hole is completed. The handicap difference here is usually based on seven-eighths of the difference in the combined team handicaps.

American Foursomes Both players from a side drive from the same tee and then hit their partner's shot before choosing the better ball to play alternately between them until the completion of the hole.

Threesome A match in which one player plays against two and each side plays one ball. The side that has two players plays alternate shots as in foursomes (*see* above).

Cricket Played by three players as a three-ball. Six points are awarded on each hole: the lowest net score per hole scores 4 points, with 2 points for the second lowest net score and nothing for third. (If second and third players tie, they get 1 point each.) If two players tie, they receive 3 points each with none for the third. If all three tie with the lowest net, then all score 2 points (or none). The full shot allowance must be used.

Four-ball – betterball In this competition, two players form a side, each playing his own ball throughout. The better net score of the partners is the score for the side. Players take three-quarters of the difference from the lowest handicapper.

Four-ball Aggregate Two players form a side. Each player plays his own ball throughout but must finish the hole. The score is the combined aggregate of each team.

Bogey/Par Each player or side plays against bogey – or par. Players score 'plus' for every hole played in net birdie or better, a 'half' for net par, and a 'minus' or 'loss' for holes played above net par. The aggregate of plusses, halves and losses is taken to give a final score of so many holes up (or down) to bogey/par.

Stableford Traditional points system. A player or a side plays against the course (that is, par for the course). Two or more over net par scores 0 points; net bogey scores 1 point; net par scores 2 points; net birdie 3 points; net eagle 4 points; and net albatross 5 points.

Murfs The points system used in the European tour's Murphy's Cup: 4 points for net eagle, 2 for birdie, 0 for par and -1 for bogey or more.

Denver Named after the international event on the US PGA Tour, this competition takes the form of a modified Stableford format: 8 points for net albatross, 5 for eagle, 2 for birdie, 0 for par, -1 for bogey and -3 for double bogey or worse.

Skins Usually played in a four-ball, players take part as individuals with the aim of winning as many 'skins' as possible ('skins' refers to bets placed by each player on a score for each hole). The individual with the lowest total on a hole wins the skin. If players tie a score, the skin is carried over to the next hole. Players can find their allegiances with their opponents switching radically through the round as they rely on players to tie the holes, thus keeping their own chances alive.

Eclectic Played over two or more strokeplay rounds. Each competitor counts his best score returned at each hole out of the two (or more) rounds. This is also known as the Ringer Competition.

GAMES FOR FUN

Then there are those competitions that are often played during festival days, or just for a lot of laughs among friends. The variations on these are infinite, and all it takes to enlarge on them is a sense of humour and a little ingenuity.

However, of all the competitions available to the golfer – professional or merely weekender – the toughest remains playing against himself. After all, golf is the ultimate test of skill and character, which is what brings us all back to the course, no matter how well or badly we've played.

Bloodsome Also goes under the name of Gruesome and Yellowsome. Two players form a side and both drive from the same tee throughout. However, their opponents pick their worst drive and the team must proceed as straight foursomes from there until the completion of the hole.

The handicap allowance here is the same as for greensomes – though from hereon, the basis on which team handicaps are arrived at will frequently be the subject of much first-tee discussion.

Texas (or American) Scramble
No guesses where this one originated. Players form teams of three or four. All players drive, and the best ball is selected by each team and then marked. All players either place (on the fairway) or drop at that point and play from there. Again the best ball is selected, and so on, until the green is reached and the hole completed. There are many handicap formulas, but the easiest is usually to add all three (or four) handicaps together and divide by 10. The team handicap is deducted at the end.

Daytona One for the gamblers; played as a four-ball but each team puts two scores together. For example, if you take 3 and 3, your team score is 33. If your rivals both take 5, their score is 55; hence you are 22 points ahead. If either team member scores par or better, the lower score goes first, i.e. a 7 and 3 on a par four would become 37. But if both members score above par, the highest score goes first, i.e. 5 and 7 becomes 75 – a swing of 38 points.

Flag Competition Each player is given a flag with his or her name on it. Proceed around the course until your score is equal to your handicap plus par, i.e. on a par 70 course, a 12-handicapper would get 70 + 12 = 82 shots. On completion of a player's 82nd shot, he or she puts the flag where the ball lies.

The winner is the player who advances his or her flag furthest around the course before his/her shot quota runs out. The best players may actually have to play the first and second holes again (their 19th and 20th).

BETTING

Betting is an integral part of the game, and is practised all over the world for varying sums. Apart from simply betting on the result of a match, the most common form of betting is called Nassau. Here players bet on the first nine holes, the second nine and then on the overall result. Variations on this are plentiful, as are the stakes.

Another immensely popular form of gambling, often played in conjunction with the above, is to play for 'units'. Units are won for myriad 'feats' such as the shot closest to the pin on short holes, par saves from bunkers, the longest drives, and birdies.

Betting on the golf course can become enormously complicated and novices should be wary of placing too much money on too many bets. Beware the unscrupulous hustlers; there are many waiting to take your hard-earned loot.

Above *A scorer at the Colonial Country Club in Fort Worth, Texas, during The Colonial Tournament in 1998.*

"NEVER BET WITH ANYONE YOU MEET ON THE FIRST TEE WHO HAS A DEEP SUNTAN, A 1-IRON IN HIS BAG AND SQUINTY EYES."

— *DAVE MARR*

Following pages *The 18th green at the Golf National club in Paris; the French Open was held here in 1998.*

1 1 9

CHAPTER SEVEN

GOLF COURSE DESIGN

MAN'S DESIGNS ON NATURE

Scotland's early links courses were shaped by nature, not man. They featured bunkers that evolved from use rather than design and the fairways consisted of areas of fine-bladed grass threading their way through the gorse.

Towards the end of the 19th century the first inland courses were built, with architects incorporating features from the best links courses and adding new ideas. Because natural hazards weren't as common on inland courses, they had to be created, the most obvious being water. Two schools of thought on golf architecture evolved:

Penal – here, a hole dictates the line of play and punishes harshly the player who strays from it;

Strategic – offers several options of varying difficulty; punishes a poor shot but rewards a good one.

Because of the size of the North American continent, inland courses became common. The first proper parkland course of significance, Oakmont, was built in 1903. The course lacked natural hazards, so 300 bunkers were created. The first true penal course, Oakmont was instrumental in establishing this school of architecture, which remained prevalent till the 1930s.

In terms of layout, the style on early courses was to form nine holes out to a point and then nine holes back. Muirfield in Scotland became the first course to depart from this norm, creating two loops of nine, which also served to vary the way holes were played relative to the prevailing wind. Between the wars, the popularity of the game soared, particularly in the USA where Bobby Jones had become a national hero.

When Augusta National in Georgia was built by Jones after his retirement, this spectacular course with its wide fairways, relatively sparse bunkering and subtle mounding was to prove the most influential of its time, demonstrating beyond a doubt the superiority of the strategic school of course design. This era between the World Wars became known as the Golden Age of golf course design, when gifted architects were given magnificent pieces of land on which to be creative.

The Lost City Country Club, at the Sun City complex in South Africa which is home to the Million Dollar Challenge.

Few courses were built in the period immediately after World War II, but during the 1950s, and coupled with the increasing popularity of American Arnold Palmer, golf again experienced a boom. Technological advances in construction machinery and irrigation systems meant that golf courses could be built on land such as desert, marshland and mountain slopes – previously unfit for the purpose. In addition, the increased mobility of the public led to an increased demand for courses in exotic holiday locations around the world, allowing developers to take advantage of spectacular settings.

As golf equipment evolved and golfers were able to hit the ball across ever increasing distances, a growing emphasis on length for golf holes became apparent. However, golfers of varying abilities were catered for with the construction of a series of tees, which offered not only variations in length but also in line of attack. The top modern architects have kept to the classic features of the masters of yesteryear, but have added their own signature features.

Although agronomy, science, engineering, forestry and geology play ever increasing roles in course design, the ultimate aim remains the same: to blend fairways and greens, sand and water, course and surroundings, into an interesting and attractive golf course, to be enjoyed by every player who ventures out onto its layout.

"I ASKED MY WIFE IF SHE WANTED A VERSACE DRESS, DIAMONDS OR PEARLS AS A PRESENT. SHE SAID, 'NO!' WHEN I ASKED HER WHAT SHE DID WANT SHE SAID, 'A DIVORCE' BUT I TOLD HER I WASN'T INTENDING TO SPEND THAT MUCH." (AFTER HE HAD WON THE MILLION DOLLAR CHALLENGE AT SUN CITY)

— *NICK FALDO*

123

The Outeniqua mountains form a spectacular backdrop to the two Gary Player-designed courses at Fancourt in the Cape, South Africa.

GARY PLAYER'S COURSE DESIGN PHILOSOPHY

Many of the world's top golfers such as Gary Player have broadened their careers into other aspects of the game of golf such as course design. The Gary Player Design Company has designed courses in 14 different countries, from Sun City in South Africa to Palm Springs in California and Chiba in Japan. Player's company has completed over 100 golf course design projects around the world.

One of Player's aims when designing a course is to make each course unique, so that a golfer will not be able to identify a specific designer's trademark. His course design philosophy combines modern technology with traditional design. A course must be versatile so that it can still challenge the skills of the world's top professionals yet also provide enjoyment for the average golfer and meet the needs of the nonprofessional. Expertise and precision take preference over power, and rewards are given for accuracy rather than distance. The use of multiple tee positions provides added versatility, as does strategic bunkering around the greens and varying the approach to the maintenance of the course.

The 1980s saw a proliferation of extremely difficult courses with particularly undulating greens that, when properly maintained, provided an almost unplayable and far too difficult putting surface for the average golfer. Player believes, however, that greens should have some undulation but that this should evolve out of the creation of plateaus which enable golfers who succeed in placing their approach shots a few metres from the pin to have a relatively predictable putt to the hole.

Another important consideration for Player is that the course should enhance the environment. Natural features of the landscape such as trees, streams and terrain variations are incorporated to create balance, beauty and harmony, which increase as the course grows older. Where the natural environment has been changed, every effort is made to reintroduce indigenous trees, grasses and water masses to attract birds and wildlife to the area. The aim is to create memorable golf holes to which golfers yearn to return.

The South African course designer also believes that vision is vital in the design of a golf course – the golfer must be able to see all of the hazards and also enjoy all the views that the topography offers.

In this regard the orientation of the holes is important, not only to keep the sun out of a golfer's eyes, but also to create interesting and beautiful shadows in the morning and evening.

A crocodile pit creates an unusual hazard at the 13th hole of the Lost City Golf Course in South Africa.

Golf equipment is improving all the time, with the result that courses designed 30 years ago are now too short for today's big hitters. Courses cannot be continually lengthened, but a clever and strategic approach to design will give a course the elasticity to stand up to the technological advances of the future.

A Hazard with a Difference Among Gary Player's more famous designs are the two golf courses at the Sun City entertainment complex in South Africa: the Gary Player Country Club and the Lost City Golf Course. The former has hosted southern Africa's biggest and best-known golf tournament, the Million Dollar Challenge, since the event's inception in 1981, while the Lost City Golf Course provides a real walk on the wild side! Among other eye-catching features of the course, the par three 13th hole requires a tee shot over a rather unusual 'hazard' – a large pit filled with crocodiles – to a green in the shape of the African continent, guarded by bunkers filled with sand of different colours.

GREAT GOLF COURSES OF THE WORLD

Ranked in the top five of the world's 100 greatest golf courses are: Augusta National in Atlanta, Georgia, USA, certainly the best known of the world's parkland courses (5th); the Old Course at St Andrews in Scotland, one of the oldest and most loved links courses (4th); and Cypress Point in California, USA, built alongside the Pacific Ocean in a truly spectacular setting (1st). And finally, the Gary Player Country Club at Sun City, a glorious parkland course cut into the harsh bushveld, is considered one of Player's most famous creations.

AUGUSTA NATIONAL

In 1930, the great Bobby Jones, at the age of 28, retired from competitive golf, having achieved in the game everything he possibly could. He planned to return to his law practice and make some money with instructional films and books, plus fulfil a long-held ambition: to found a golf club with a superior course, near his home in Georgia, where he could play with his friends. Jones himself chose the site for Augusta National and commissioned a professional golf course architect to design it – Dr Alister Mackenzie, a Scotsman who was also responsible for other famous layouts such as Cypress Point in California and Royal Melbourne in Australia.

Between them, Jones and Mackenzie came up with a course that had broad fairways, nonexistent rough, and greens that were manageable (although they are less so today when cut very short for tournament play). The area was blessed with an almost

Above *The green at Augusta's par three 12th is guarded by water and bunkers.*
Opposite top *Crowds surround the greens of Augusta's 6th and 16th holes during the US Masters.*

The par five 13th forms the last leg of the notorious 'Amen Corner' at Augusta.

endless variety of plants and flowers and it was later decided to name each hole after a particular species – Azalea, Redbud, Magnolia, and so on. The course is a blaze of colour each year in springtime. It is undoubtedly the best known course in America, and when the azaleas are flowering, one of the most beautiful golf courses in the world. The Masters, the first of the modern Majors on the world golfing cal-

endar, was begun in 1934 and is played at Augusta in April each year. Gary Player has won the Masters on three occasions – in 1961, 1974 and 1978 – and in fact names his 1978 victory as his greatest moment in golf (*see* 18 Memorable Moments, page 136). Player has this to say about the course:

'Augusta – or rather Bobby Jones and Alister Mackenzie who designed it – got golf's equation exactly right in that the player is allowed a selection of strategies and is then rewarded or punished in proportion to the degree of skill displayed.

'You stand on the tee and gaze at those wide fairways and think you will kill it. But it is not that easy. In a clever way, Augusta allows you to create your own problems. The trouble is obvious and avoidable. It is the element of risk – and the bad shot – that makes people come to grief. The secret of Augusta is the narrowness – from front to back – of its greens. They are wide enough but have very little depth, which means they demand absolute

precision, even with short irons. In these terms, the short 12th – which forms part of the notorious Amen Corner stretch of crucial homeward holes – is perhaps the perfect par three. It measures 155 yards and requires no more than an eight-iron or a seven-iron, and yet it has ruined many winning chances because the green is virtually a narrow strip between bunkers at the rear and water in the front. After all, anyone can create a difficult par three by making it excessively long. But it takes skill and imagination to produce such a formidable test as this one with more modest dimensions.

'Its true accolade is that it is the sort of hole you worry about before you even get there. It is a fearsome challenge, not least because of its sequence in the round at Amen Corner. A bad shot would almost certainly mean a double bogey.'

ST ANDREWS (OLD COURSE)
The Old Course at the Royal and Ancient Golf Club of St Andrews (R&A) in Scotland, known as the home of golf, is one of the world's oldest and most revered. No-one knows when golf was first played at St Andrews, but the first records date back to 1552 and the Old Course remains as a monument to the origins of golf, as a game played on links by the sea.

The first tee and the 18th green of the Old Course are overlooked by the imposing façade of the headquarters of the R&A which came into existence in 1754. Ten years later the R&A instructed that the number of holes on the Old Course be

One of the most famous views in golf – the bridge over the Swilcan Burn, with St Andrews in the background.

Previous pages *Sunlight sparkles off the Firth of Clyde at the 8th hole of the Ailsa Course at Turnberry Golf Club, on Scotland's west coast.*

The green and the road (right) and bunker (below) at the infamous Road Hole, the par four 17th on the Old Course at St Andrews.

reduced from 22 to 18, an arrangement that became the standard when the club emerged as the arbiter of golfing rules and format.

In all the years since the Old Course was formed, its outline has never changed – the S-shaped layout has the traditional form of nine holes out and nine back and the course still has the unusual feature of seven huge double, or shared, greens.

Since 1873, St Andrews has hosted the British Open on 28 occasions and has seen players of the calibre of Bobby Jones, Sam Snead, Peter Thomson, Bobby Locke, Jack Nicklaus (on two occasions), Seve Ballesteros and Nick Faldo lift the coveted Claret Jug. St Andrews will again host the British Open in the year 2000.

Among the course's more famous holes is the 17th, commonly known as the Road Hole, a 461yd (421m) par four. This is one of only four holes that does not feature a double green and the hole's single green, guarded by one of the most feared bunkers in the game, has long proved an elusive target to golfers, from amateurs to the top professionals. The tee shot at the 17th is played alongside a road on the right, while the Old Course Hotel, formerly a railway yard, forms out-of-bounds to the right of the fairway. A road runs behind the green, which is guarded on the left by the infamous Road Hole bunker. The bunker is deep, with steep sides, and has ruined many a scorecard. Tommy Nakajima took four strokes to get out of the bunker, eventually carding a 9 here in the 1978 British Open, after which it became known as 'the Sands of Nakajima'.

CYPRESS POINT

Gary Player rates this course as one of his favourite throughout the world:

'For its scenic splendour and a unique completeness, Cypress Point on the rugged Californian coastline close to Pebble Beach and Monterey is a favourite. It is the complete golf course because its terrain offers a hint of parkland which expands into a form of heathland and then a stretch of links by the sea, thus combining all forms of golf as we know it. It is a magical spot and contains one of golf's most famous holes – the short 16th where tee and green are perched on either side of a cove above the raging Pacific Ocean. The brave man bids for the green knowing full well the penalties of failure. His cautious opponent settles for a mid-iron along the clifftop with the outside hope of a chip and putt

Left *The clubhouse and the town of St Andrews form a backdrop to the Old Course's par four 18th hole.*

The spectacular par three 16th at Cypress Point in California is played over the raging Pacific Ocean.

Above *The tee at Cypress Point's par three 16th is set on a rugged rocky outcrop above the ocean.*

Right *Cypress Point's par three 15th.*

to save his par. It remains, therefore, the classic example of strategic golf.'

Cypress Point is situated around 90 miles (150km) south of San Francisco at the tip of the Monterey Peninsula, a rugged piece of land jutting out into the Pacific Ocean. The Peninsula is also home to Cypress Point's more illustrious neighbour, Pebble Beach. While Pebble Beach has hosted the US Open on three occasions, the only event of any significance that is held at Cypress Point is the annual National Pebble Beach Pro-Am, which draws a host of celebrities, from movie stars and pop singers to former US presidents, who team up to play with the US PGA Tour professionals. The Pro-Am tournament is played over three courses: Cypress Point, Pebble Beach and the relatively new Spyglass Hill.

It is often claimed that Cypress Point is one of the loveliest golf courses ever built – waves batter the tall cliffs, sea lions bask on the rocks just offshore and fishing boats dot the ocean surface.

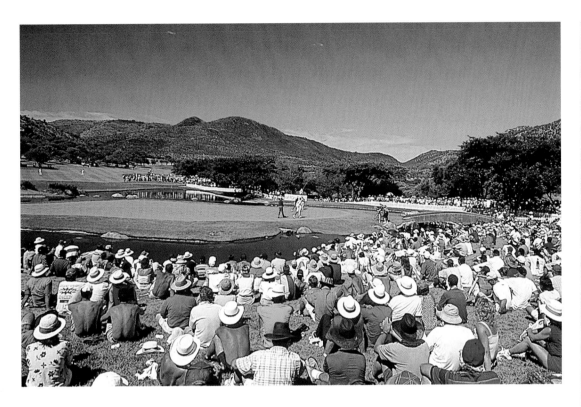

GARY PLAYER COUNTRY CLUB

Gary Player's creation at Sun City annually hosts the biggest event on Southern Africa's golfing calendar – the Million Dollar Challenge. The event was inaugurated in 1981 by South African entrepreneur Sol Kerzner after a suggestion from Lee Trevino that the resort sponsor a tournament with a million-dollar purse, and at the time, the winners read like a who's who of world golf: Johnny Miller, Ray Floyd, Seve Ballesteros, Bernhard Langer, Mark McNulty, Ian Woosnam, Fulton Allem, David Frost, Nick Price, Nick Faldo, Corey Pavin and Colin Montgomerie. Player describes what he set out to achieve:

'What a golf course needs is what I call elasticity, not simply in terms of being stretched to accommodate the long-hitters, but in displaying a variety of tees with bunkers designed to challenge them. Thus a golf course must be all things to all men. It must be flexible enough to provide a varying challenge for the old lady golfer, the young player and the top professional.... In 1979, I was given the specific task of building one of the toughest golf courses in the world as the venue for the Million Dollar Challenge at Sun City: it was intended to test the greatest players in the game for what was

the biggest first prize in world golf. At the same time, I also designed alternative tees to accommodate the holidaymakers who visit this resort.'

Undoubtedly the most exciting hole on the course is the par five 9th, a long par five with just one large bunker – on the right and in the landing area of the tee shot. The hole curves left to a spectacular island green rising out of a dam with Sun City in the background. 'The ninth can be classified as a heroic par five,' says Player, 'even though it is regularly set up to allow golfers to reach the green on their second shot. This is a hole where a swing of two or three shots can easily occur.'

The Gary Player Country Club's 9th hole: when played from the front tee, it is a classic risk-reward par five. The green is reachable in two shots – thereby setting up an eagle opportunity, or a birdie – but this involves a long, risky approach shot over water.

Top and left *The par five 9th at Sun City during the Million Dollar Challenge.*

133

CHAPTER EIGHT

18 MEMORABLE MOMENTS

GARY'S GREATEST MOMENT

Recorded in Gary Player's own words: 'It was recently pointed out to me that my victories in Major championships span five decades, the first being the British Open in 1959 and the most recent the 1997 Wentworth Masters in London. I was tempted to call this my greatest moment, but that would be stretching the meaning of the moment quite considerably. Rather, I cast my mind back to the first week of April 1978, a day I can remember as clearly as if it were yesterday.

'It was the final day of the 1978 US Masters at Augusta, Georgia. I was seven shots behind going into the last round. My son Wayne was with me that morning and I can recall him saying: "You know dad, you're playing so well, if you putt well today you might shoot 64 and win." Going out I shot 34. Hope faded. To win I would have to beat not only the field on the day, but every golfer in living history – no-one had ever succeeded in shooting a 30 at Augusta on the last day to win.

' "Never say never" had never been so true. I came back in 30 and won the tournament. I was playing with Severiano Ballesteros and when I won

Watson helping Player put on the green jacket in 1978.

he walked across the green and gave me a huge hug. Later he went on to say that I taught him how to win the Masters, which I thought was a lovely compliment coming from a great player like himself. At that stage I was the oldest player ever to have won the Masters. It was a wonderful feeling at the age of 42, playing against all the younger stars, to win a Major championship – one of golf's most important at that.

'In the following week in the Tournament of Champions in California, I was once again seven behind going into the last round. I shot 65 and beat Seve Ballesteros who was seven ahead of me. The next week I went to Houston, Texas. I was five behind the leader, Andy Bean. Being a jovial, giant

Spectators study the scoreboard at the 1919 British Open at St Andrews, Scotland.

FROM TEARS TO TRIUMPH

As the 1959 British Open at Muirfield reached its climax, 23-year-old Gary Player turned from the 18th green in tears. Player was convinced that he had thrown away the greatest opportunity of his young life: victory in his first Major and the world's most prestigious championship. Player had opened the tournament badly, carding a 75 to trail the leaders by 7 shots. His round-two score was 4 shots lower, but was only 2 inside the qualifying score of 148. He got only 1 stroke lower on day three, shooting 70 for a total of 216, but was still 4 behind the leaders, the UK's Fred Bullock and Sam King, and there was a total of 13 players with scores equal to or better than his. But he still felt he could do it. Player made a promising start to his final round, going out in 34, and it appeared that he was going to make it back in 32 for a 66 and a realistic shot at the title. But he bunkered his drive and then three-putted on the 18th to drop 2 shots and slip to 68 and a total of 284. An interminably long wait followed and the leaders dropped off, one by one, Bullock and Belgian Flory van Donck finishing on 286.

A tearful Player, convinced he had lost, was being comforted by his wife Vivienne when officials approached to tell him he had just become the youngest champion since Willie Auchterlonie in 1893.

of a man, he came over to me and said: "Well, you sawn-off little runt, you're not going to beat me. You may have won the last two from seven behind, but you ain't gonna do it again!" I shot 64 in the final round and beat him as well.

'That made me the only player ever to have won three in a row including a Major tournament. This record still stands on the PGA Tour today. A Major championship is like winning Wimbledon. To win just once in your life is quite something. But after being a runner-up three times, to win your third Masters (once in the Sixties, twice in the Seventies) and then go on to crown it by winning the next two tournaments as well... it is a great honour and certainly my most memorable moment in golf.'

Player's first Major: the 1959 British Open, played at Muirfield.

Francis Ouimet with his young caddie, Eddie Lowery, at the US Open in 1913.

OUIMET THE GIANT KILLER

Although the US Open was America's national title, the event was dominated by Scottish and English professionals in the late 19th century and first decade of the 20th century. The first American to win the tournament was Johnny McDermott, in 1911 (he won again in 1912), but it was the 1913 victory by 20-year-old Francis de Sales Ouimet, an amateur who worked at a sporting goods store, that provided the spark for an American golf explosion. The young underdog's victory – he was the first amateur to win the event – captured the imagination of the US sporting public and he was dubbed the 'World's Golf Champion' by the *New York Times*.

Ouimet was 20 when, on his fourth attempt, he gained entry to the US Open, held that year at The Country Club in Brookline, Massachusetts. The course was across the road from the Ouimet family home and the young man had worked there as a caddie in earlier years. At the time, Johnny McDermott was America's hope to repel the powerful two-pronged challenge from the UK's Harry Vardon and Ted Ray. A crowd of over 10,000 braved heavy rain as the Open entered an unprecedented fifth day. Ouimet, the local hero, played steadily from tee to green using the less common interlocking grip rather than the overlapping grip that Vardon had popularized, while his more experienced opponents made one error after another. The trio were level after nine holes, but on the 10th both Englishmen three-putted and Ouimet was ahead to stay. On the par four 17th his birdie put him in the lead by 3 shots, which he increased to 5 on the 18th.

Ouimet made the front pages around the country – as did his caddie, 10-year-old Eddie Lowery, who had had to fight off suggestions that a more experienced caddie should have been accompanying Ouimet. Lowery won, and his constant advice to Ouimet to keep his eye on the ball paid off.

The logo designed for the 100th US Open held at Brookline in 1995 was based on a silhouette from a photograph of Ouimet with little Eddie Lowery at his side.

JONES'S 'IMPREGNABLE QUADRILATERAL'

Bobby Jones was born in Atlanta, Georgia, in 1902 and by the age of 20 had become a golfing phenomenon. In his brief career in the decade up to and including 1930, he played only 52 tournaments, either amateur or professional, and won 23 of them, including four US Opens, five US Amateurs, three British Opens and one British Amateur. His golfing calendar was light – he played only a handful of events a year, apart from friendly club four-balls on weekends, taking the winter off and warming up in spring with a few practice balls.

Merion Golf Club in Pennsylvania has hosted several US Opens and US Amateurs, but its first real claim to fame came in 1930 when it was the scene of the final act of Bobby Jones's Grand Slam. Merion's 11th is, at 370yd (338m), a short par four. Jones was 8 up on Gene Homans in the final of the US Amateur. His drive found the fairway, he hit the green with his second and he two-putted for par to halve the hole and win the event 8 and 7. This title, with his victories in the British Amateur at St Andrews, the British Open at Hoylake and the US Open at Interlaken (at the time accepted as the four Major championships) made Jones the first player to win all four titles in the same season, a feat dubbed the 'Impregnable Quadrilateral'.

Shortly after his 1930 Grand Slam, having achieved everything he could in the game, Jones retired from competitive golf at the age of 28. He

Bobby Jones with the trophies of (from left): the British Open (the Claret Jug), US Amateur, British Amateur and US Open championships.

planned to return to his law practice plus fulfil a long-held ambition: to found a golf club with a superior course in Georgia. That course was Augusta National and the first Augusta National Invitation event was held in 1934, the tournament that became known as the Masters.

Diminutive Gene Sarazen.

SARAZEN'S ALBATROSS

It was dubbed 'the shot that was heard around the world'. The scene was the 1935 US Masters, only the second time the event had been played. American Gene Sarazen, 3 strokes off the lead – held by Craig Wood, who was just finishing his final round – was playing his second shot at the par five 15th at Augusta National. 'Mr Gene, you got to hit the 3-wood if you want to clear that water,' said Stovepipe, Sarazen's caddie. But the farmer from Connecticut opted for a 4-wood. Sarazen had played his drive about 250yd (229m) into damp grass on the right-hand side of the fairway. His 4-wood shot flew low and a little to the right, but kicked left and into the hole for an albatross (also known as a double eagle), and with that single stroke he erased Wood's 3-shot lead. He was the only player on the course who could have caught Wood; the latter was already being photographed and congratulated when news of 'the shot' came through.

Sarazen went on to par the remaining four holes to finish tied with Wood on 282. In the 36-hole play-off the following day, Sarazen played faultless golf to prevail by 5 strokes, 144 to 149, adding a US Masters victory to the six Major titles he already held (the 1922 US Open and US PGA Championship, at age 20; the 1923 US PGA; the 1932 British Open and US Open; and the 1933 US PGA). He became the first person to complete the professional Grand Slam of all four Major titles.

HOGAN'S HEROIC RETURN

American Ben Hogan is the only golfer to have won three Majors in one year – that was 1953, when he triumphed in the US Masters, the US Open and the British Open, his ninth and last Major title. But success hadn't come easy for Hogan. His father, a

Hogan recovered from severe injuries in a motor vehicle accident to win the 1950 US Open.

blacksmith, died when Ben was 10 and his mother moved to Fort Worth, Texas. Here, Hogan sold newspapers and was introduced to the game of golf at Glen Garden Country Club, where he worked as a caddie. He turned professional in 1931 at the age of 19, but it was not until 1940 that he began to find real success on the tour. In that same year and the two that followed, he was the leading prize money winner, but his career was interrupted in 1942 when he was called away for military service.

After the war, Hogan emerged as a supreme talent, winning 21 times in the first two seasons, including his first Major, the 1946 US PGA Championship. In 1948 he went on to win two Majors, his second

US PGA title and the US Open. Then tragedy struck. In 1949, he was injured in a car accident that put him out of the game for more than a year. Many thought he'd never play again, but he returned in 1950, though walking was agony, and restricted himself to a few events, focusing on the Majors.

The 1950 US Open brought one of the most memorable moments in this great golfer's career – and in the history of the game. Just 16 months after the accident, Hogan stood on the tee of the 72nd hole, the long and difficult par four 18th at Merion Golf Club, his legs wracked with pain. He had let slip a 3-stroke lead, dropping shots on the 12th, 15th and 17th, and was tied with Lloyd Mangrum and George Fazio who had just finished up ahead of him. A par would put him in the play-off for the title.

Hogan's tee shot found the fairway, but he was still faced with an approach of over 200yd (183m) on the 445yd (407m) hole. The crowd lining the fairway fell silent as he reached for his 1-iron. He took his stance and played one of the most famous shots of all time, his ball landing in the centre of the green. Hogan two-putted for par and a tie for the play-off. The next day he returned, revitalized, to outplay Fazio and Mangrum and claim his second US Open.

CONTROVERSY AT LOCKE'S LAST OPEN

South African Bobby Locke was the first golfer to dominate on three continents – at home as well as in the USA and Europe. Locke, who had been enjoying a hugely successful career at home and building a reputation as one of the finest putters ever, invited American Sam Snead to an exhibition tour of singles matchplay following Snead's victory in the 1946 British Open. Locke won 12 of the 16 matches; Snead, amazed at the South African's putting skills, suggested that he try his luck in the USA. Locke was very successful there, finishing second on the

South Africa's Bobby Locke won four British Opens over a nine-year period.

money list in 1947 and winning three times in 1948 before the US PGA banned him from their events for 'failing to honour' his playing contracts.

He decided to spend more time playing in Europe and he began to be a dominant force in the British Open, winning at Sandwich in 1949, at Troon in 1950 and at Lytham in 1952.

Locke's fourth and last success came in the 1957 Open Championship at St Andrews, a victory that was briefly clouded by a controversial incident but which proved to be a defining moment in the history of the game. Over a period of 10 years, from 1949 to 1958, Locke had dominated the Open with Australian Peter Thomson – only Englishman Max Faulkner (1951) and American Ben Hogan (1953) broke the pair's run of victories, and it was Thomson that Locke defeated in 1957. Locke went into the final round 3 shots ahead of Thomson and Scotsman Eric Brown, and a round of 70 saw him home. (Thomson, attempting to emulate Young Tom Morris's four in a row, had also come home in 70 to lose by three strokes.)

However, on the 72nd and final hole of the tournament, the incident took place: Locke, whose ball lay about 3ft (1m) from the hole, moved his marker one putter-head-length to allow his playing partner a clear putt, as is allowed in the Rules of Golf. His partner three-putted and then Locke, in the excitement of imminent victory, forgot to replace his marker in its original resting place before two-putting for a par four and a 3-stroke victory.

Bobby Locke was presented with the trophy and it was only later, on newsreel film, that the error was noticed. According to the rules of the game, Locke had played the ball from the incorrect position, for which a two-stroke penalty is awarded. Locke had then signed his card for a 4 on the final hole – an incorrect score – for which the penalty is, unfortunately, disqualification.

The Championship Committee smoothly defused the controversy by announcing that Locke had gained no advantage from his failure to replace his marker and that the result would stand, with Locke being permitted to retain his Open Championship title. The Committee's respect both for Bobby Locke and for the game of golf, and their decision to override the rules for the good of the game, is a historically significant moment.

DE VICENZO'S FATAL ERROR

The flick of a pencil ruined an Easter birthday for 45-year-old Argentinian Roberto de Vicenzo on 14 April 1968, the final day of the 32nd US Masters. De Vicenzo was already in the television interview room, in anticipation of tying with American Bob Goalby and forcing a Monday play-off for the title, when he received the tragic news. Earlier, Goalby had carded a final round of 66 for a total of 277 while De Vicenzo shot a 65 to match

Argentinian Roberto de Vicenzo.

this total. But the latter's playing partner, Tommy Aaron, had accidentally marked a 4 instead of a 3 on the scorecard for him on the 71st hole, the par four 17th (the Argentinian had holed his 5ft, or 1.5m, birdie putt). And De Vicenzo had signed the card. The rules of the game state that if a player returns a score higher than he actually achieved, the score stands (if De Vicenzo had signed for a lower score than he had actually shot he would have been disqualified). This meant that De Vicenzo was credited with a final round of 66 and a total of 278 – one shot out of a play-off – and Goalby was handed the title.

'Under the Rules of Golf', came the announcement from Hord Hardin, president of the US Golf Association and chairman of the Rules Committee, 'he (Roberto de Vicenzo) will be charged with a sixty-six which does not leave him in a tie with Bob Goalby, who is eleven under par. He is second, ten under par.'

Aaron, extremely upset, rushed to his car and sped away. He said later, 'I realized I had made an error before I left the official table. I looked around for Roberto, but he was gone. There was a general state of confusion.'

De Vicenzo blamed himself and not Aaron for the mistake and tearfully uttered the immortal words: 'What a stupid I am!'

STEP ASIDE FOR SE RI PAK

Ladies' golf, although fiercely competitive, has always lived in the shadow of the men's game. Prize money is smaller, media coverage is thinner, sponsorships are

Se Ri Pak celebrates her first US victory in the McDonald's LPGA Championship in 1998.

harder to come by, and real stars are few and far between, though this has changed in the late 1990s.

Enter Se Ri Pak, a fresh-faced youngster from South Korea who joined the US LPGA (United States Ladies Professional Golf Association) Tour a month after her 20th birthday. With a sponsorship from Samsung that made LPGA regulars gasp, and a beagle puppy called Happy tucked under her arm, Pak rewrote the LPGA record books and captivated the golf world with her talents. Pak qualified for the tough US LPGA Tour on her first attempt, tying for first in the final qualifying event.

Six months later she recorded her first victory on the Tour – in an LPGA Major, the McDonald's LPGA Championship – becoming the first rookie in 10 years to record a debut victory in a Major. Pak became an overnight hero in South Korea where the event was televised live. The president phoned her before her final round, but she respectfully said she'd call him back later.

Pak's second Tour victory was also a Major; she became the youngest woman to win the US Women's Open, and the first rookie in 14 years to win two Majors. The following week she won the Kroger Classic, a fortnight later the Giant Eagle LPGA Classic, where her 23-under-par total equalled the lowest in LPGA history.

Known as the 'peacock of the fairways' for his colourful clothing, Doug Sanders was not in fine feather in the 1970 British Open.

FOUR FEET TO DESPAIR

While the history of golf is filled with memorable moments of celebration and success, there are also haunting moments of despair and missed opportunity. One such tale is that of American golfer Doug Sanders who, although he won 19 times on the US Tour between 1956 and 1972, will always be remembered for one terrible, never-to-be-forgotten shot: a missed putt of 4ft (1.2m) that cost him the British Open title.

Although he'd had a number of victories, Sanders had never won a Major and, coming into the 1970 British Open, he was past his prime and had to pre-qualify. But he was a master of improvised shots and he found the St Andrews Old Course layout to his liking. After three gusty, stormy days, American Lee Trevino led the field, with Sanders, Jack Nicklaus and Briton Tony Jacklin tied two shots back.

On the final day the wind was gusting worse than ever, and Trevino and Jacklin dropped away as Nicklaus took the lead and set a target of 283. Sanders seemed set to beat Nicklaus's score thanks to a superb save from the deep, steep-sided Road Hole bunker, his ball landing 1ft (30cm) from the hole. All he needed to win the championship was a par on the 18th, which happened to be the easiest par four on the course.

Sanders had no problems with his tee shot, but his approach was a little long. His putt down and then up the slope of the green finished 4ft (1.2m) short of the hole. To seal victory and become the first pre-qualifier to win the Open, what was required of him was simply to sink the four-footer; it was every golfer's dream – and nightmare.

Sanders took his stance and then, in mid-putt, he bent down to move a blade of grass from the line of the putt. Every golfer in the crowd was whispering, 'Step back, regain your composure, start again'. But Sanders putted immediately and the ball slid past the right of the hole.

The bogey on 18 left Sanders tied on 283 and facing Nicklaus in an 18-hole play-off the next day. Nicklaus made no mistake, winning 73–72 to claim his second British Open title.

Sanders was asked recently if the missed putt still preyed on his mind. His reply:

'No, sometimes I don't think about it for five minutes.'

"WE'VE HAD IT EASY. WHEN IT BLOWS HERE, EVEN THE SEAGULLS WALK."
(AFTER A CALM DAY AT ST ANDREWS)
— NICK FALDO

SHOOT-OUT AT TURNBERRY

The 1977 British Open played at Turnberry produced one of the greatest head-to-head battles in championship golf between US players Jack

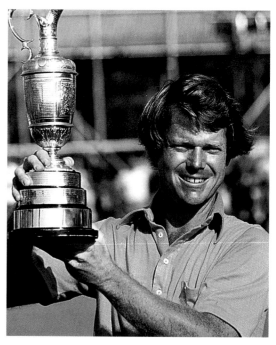

Young Tom Watson holds aloft the Claret Jug after winning the 1977 British Open.

Nicklaus, aged 37, and Tom Watson, aged 27. There was more than just the world's most prestigious title at stake; the World Number One spot hung in the balance. As a young man, Nicklaus had dethroned Arnold Palmer as the world's top golfer. Now the young Watson threatened to do the same to him.

Both players opened with rounds of 68 and 70 for a total of 138 after two rounds, one shot off the lead held by fellow American Roger Maltbie, and both players then shot 65 in the third round, pulling well clear of the rest of the field.

After Jack Nicklaus joked to the press that he wanted 'another notch on my gun', newspapers billed the final day as a showdown between the Old Gunslinger and Billy the Kid. Huge galleries, a record turnout for Scotland, flocked to the Ailsa course, so-named after Ailsa Craig, a brooding pinnacle of rock jutting from the sea alongside the Ayrshire coast.

Nicklaus made his intentions clear early on, pulling 3 shots clear in the first four holes. Watson fought back, birdying the 5th, 7th and 8th to pull level. But a dropped shot at Bruce's Castle, Turnberry's Lighthouse hole, saw Nicklaus go 1 shot clear after 9: Nicklaus out in 33, Watson in 34.

Nicklaus pulled 2 ahead at the 12th, sinking an 8yd (7.5m) putt, but Watson pulled 1 back on the 13th and then levelled the scores on the par three 15th with a startling birdie. While Nicklaus's tee shot found the green, Watson's ball landed in the light rough to the left of the green, some 40yd (37m) from the hole. Incredibly, Watson's putt found the hole and a stunned Nicklaus missed his birdie attempt. The par five 17th saw Watson pull 1 ahead – he found the green with his second, while Nicklaus hit his approach fat. Nicklaus then chipped to within 5ft (1.5m), but missed the putt for par, while Watson two-putted for birdie.

On the par four 18th Watson played safe, hitting a straight 1-iron, while Nicklaus gambled, and drove his tee shot into the gorse. Watson's superb approach shot finished a mere 2ft (60cm) from the hole, but Nicklaus powered his way out of the rough to land 12yd (11m) from the hole, from where he sunk his birdie putt. Watson briskly tapped in his putt for birdie and his second Open title.

SEVE FROM THE CAR PARK

The world first heard the name Severiano Ballesteros in 1976, when the 19-year-old Spaniard tied for the lead with a 69 in the first round of the British Open.

The next day he shot another 69 to take a 2-shot lead, and after day three he led by the same margin over US player Johnny Miller. The next day, however, Miller soon moved ahead as Ballesteros hit more than his usual share of wild shots. But a late flurry saw him finish second, and the world knew it would be seeing more of Seve Ballesteros.

His moment of glory came three years later in the 1979 British Open at Royal Lytham, Blackpool. Seve's scores reflected his erratic genius, his wayward driving and remarkable recovery shots, as he recorded a 10-shot difference between his second and third round scores. Of his final round, Joe Gergen of *Newsday* wrote: 'Ballesteros forged a new path to glory. It hooked left and then sliced right. It

dipped and detoured through sand and scrub. It meandered through bushes and across cart tracks and even into a parking lot…'

He hit the fairway once in nine attempts with his driver. Seve's fame for wild play was cemented on the 16th hole when his drive flew so far right it landed in the car park where the BBC leave their vehicles. It was not out-of-bounds, and Seve got a free drop. He hit a sand wedge to 5yd (4.5m) from the pin and sunk the putt for a birdie.

Up ahead on 18, Jack Nicklaus, 2 off the lead at 2 over par and the only player who could beat Seve, was contemplating his chances of a birdie as he lined up his approach shot. A roar came from the 16th

Spaniard Seve Ballesteros was one of the greatest 'escape artists' the game has ever seen.

followed by another as a red '1' appeared next to the name of Ballesteros on the scoreboard at 18. Nicklaus hit into the bunker. Although he managed to save par, he finished as runner-up for the seventh time, tied for second with Ben Crenshaw 3 behind Seve Ballesteros.

Ballesteros became the first Spaniard to lift the Claret Jug and the first player from the European continent to win the Open since Arnaud Massy in 1907. 'I play good from the rough', he said afterwards. 'I have plenty of practice.'

RYDER CUP GLORY

The first Ryder Cup match between the USA and Britain and Ireland was played in 1927 and, during the 22 matches held between then and 1977, the American advantage in points scored surpassed three figures. In 1979, the Ryder Cup was played for

Scotland's Sam Torrance raises his arms in triumph on the 18th green at The Belfry in the UK after sinking the winning putt in the 1983 Ryder Cup.

the first time between Europe and the USA, and the events seemed to be following the usual pattern, with the USA winning by 6 points in 1979, and in

1981 by 9 points. But 1983 turned out to be different – the Europeans came within a putt or two of beating the Americans on their own soil, eventually losing by a slender point, a score that helped sell tickets for the 1985 showdown at the British PGA's headquarters, The Belfry in Warwickshire, UK.

The Belfry course boasts two of the toughest finishing holes in golf – the 17th is a long dogleg to an elevated green and the 18th is a par four where both the first and second shots are played over huge water hazards to a three-tiered green that demands accurate length.

The European team, with six Major titles between its members and led by nonplaying captain Tony Jacklin, started hesitantly against (nonplaying) Lee Trevino's squad which boasted 12 Majors, trailing 3½ to 4½ after the first day. Day two saw a European counterattack take Jacklin's men into a 9–7 lead, and needed 5½ points from the singles on the final day to ensure victory.

Inexperienced Spaniard Manuel Pinero got the Europeans off to a flying start, beating Lanny Wadkins 3 and 1, Englishman Paul Way beat Ray Floyd, Seve Ballesteros got a half from Tom Kite, the UK's Sandy Lyle beat Peter Jacobsen and Germany's Bernhard Langer beat Hal Sutton. That gave the Europeans 4½ points and set the stage for big-hitting Scotsman Sam Torrance.

Torrance drew level with his opponent Andy North with the 18th to play. North put his drive into the water while Torrance blasted well over the water with his drive, and his second found the right part of the green. Torrance stood, arms outstretched, as his 6yd (5.5m) birdie putt sank and he clinched victory for Europe.

'I cried all the way from the 18th tee to the green', he said afterwards. 'I knew I had won the Cup for us. I have dreamt of this all my life.'

The 16½ to 11½ victory was only the fourth time in 26 matches that the Americans had lost, and the first time they had been parted from the cup since Dai Rees's Britain and Ireland team won in 1957. The Concorde thundered overhead while 27,000 spectators and all of Europe celebrated in an emotional moment as Jacklin's team was handed the trophy.

The first Ryder Cup on European soil in 1997, at Valderrama, Spain, saw a 14½–13½ result in favour of the 'home' team.

DON'T MESS WITH THE BEAR

The 'Golden Bear' was growling. It was the run-up to the 1986 US Masters and Jack Nicklaus, aged 46 and without a doubt the greatest golfer ever, was

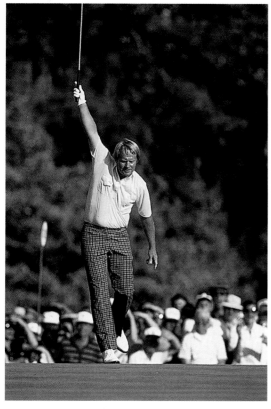

Nicklaus holes a birdie putt on the 16th, on his way to victory in the 1986 US Masters at Augusta.

being bombarded with questions: 'When will you step down, retire?' One newspaper article was the final straw according to Nicklaus: 'It said I was dead, washed up, through, with no chance whatsoever to win again. I was sizzling.' Four days later Nicklaus silenced his critics forever with one of the greatest performances in golfing history.

Playing what he said was 'the finest golf of my career', Nicklaus, who started the final round 5 strokes off the lead, launched a thunderous charge to win a record sixth Masters by 1 stroke, becoming the oldest player ever to win the event. (Previously, the oldest was Gary Player in 1978, at 42.) Nicklaus shot a magnificent 7 under par final round of 65 to collect his sixth green jacket, 23 years after he

collected his first. In doing so he beat three of the world's top players: Seve Ballesteros, feeling the pressure, found the water at the 15th; Tom Kite missed three birdie opportunities in a row; while Greg Norman birdied four straight holes to pull level with Nicklaus only to lose with a bogey on 18.

'I'm not going to quit, guys,' Nicklaus grinned to the pressmen afterwards. 'I hate to ruin your stories. Maybe I should say goodbye. Maybe that'd be the smart thing to do. But I'm not that smart. And I can still play a bit at times.'

And how! In another incredible performance, 12 years later, at the 1998 US Masters, a 58-year-old Jack Nicklaus again found himself in the running on the final nine. This time he didn't win, instead finishing a superb sixth, but there was no doubt that the front-runners felt the Bear's hot breath down their necks that Sunday afternoon. (In the same event, at the age of 62, Gary Player became the oldest golfer ever to make the cut at the US Masters.)

EUROPE WINS ON US SOIL

Excitement reached fever pitch during the last few hours of the 1987 Ryder Cup as Europe registered its first win on American soil. The venue was Jack Nicklaus's first great masterpiece of course design, Muirfield Village, not far from his birthplace in Columbus, Ohio, and Nicklaus was the home team captain. It was the first time the event had been covered by live television in the USA and there was a sellout crowd of 25,000 to watch the final day on the beautiful course. At least 3000 European spectators had made the trip across the Atlantic to support Jacklin's team.

The first morning saw the USA take the lead in all four foursomes, to win only two, Spaniards Seve Ballesteros and José Maria Olazábal fighting back from 2 down against Larry Nelson and Payne Stewart, and Briton Nick Faldo and Welshman Ian Woosnam pulling off a spectacular recovery from 4 down against Larry Mize and Lanny Wadkins. Europe won all the afternoon fourballs, with Woosnam getting lucky on the 11th when his ball flew wide, hit a tree and rebounded onto the green from where he holed for eagle. Jacklin's men found themselves 6–2 ahead after day one.

The second morning's foursomes went to Europe 2½ to 1½ and the USA could only manage to square

European team captain Tony Jacklin celebrates a Ryder Cup victory on US soil in 1987.

the afternoon's matches at 2–2 to put the tally at 10½ to 5½ with the singles to play. The Americans needed 9 of the 12 points on day three to win and they made a run for it. Jacklin needed 4 points for victory, and he was struggling. The UK's Howard Clark beat Dan Pohl at the last and Scotland's Sam Torrance held on to a half against Masters champion Mize, but Langer was struggling and down went Woosnam, Faldo, Lyle and José Rivero.

Then Ireland's Eamonn Darcy came to the rescue. He had never won a Ryder Cup match in 10 starts, but he beat Ben Crenshaw with a key birdie at the 17th, set up by a superb 6-iron approach. Langer recovered to halve with Nelson, Ballesteros beat Curtis Strange, and Scotland's Gordon Brand added a half against Wadkins to give Europe victory by 15 to 13, the USA's first defeat on home soil and only their fifth ever loss in 27 matches.

A tearful Ben Crenshaw embraces his wife after an emotional victory in the 1995 US Masters.

TOUCHED BY AN ANGEL
As 'Gentle Ben' Crenshaw sunk his final putt to win his second US Masters in 1995, he fell to his knees and broke down in tears. Eight days earlier, on the Sunday at the beginning of Masters week, Harvey Penick, Crenshaw's much-loved coach and mentor, and one of the greatest instructors the game has known, had passed away at the age of 90. Penick had coached the 43-year-old Crenshaw for all of 37 years

and was one of the chief influences in moulding the youngster into one of the world's best players.

Crenshaw had been struggling with his game, and had missed the cut in three of his last four events. Just two weeks before the Masters, Penick had given his out-of-form protégé – known as one of the modern game's great putters – a putting lesson. Crenshaw was already in Augusta preparing for the tournament when Penick died, and on the Wednesday, the day before the Masters began, he flew back to Penick's hometown, Austin, Texas, to serve as pallbearer.

Crenshaw returned tired, emotional, and with a partially dislocated toe – hardly the condition in which to deal with the rigours of Major championship golf. But Gentle Ben eased round Augusta's green pastures in a mere 274 strokes – 14 under par – to pip another Penick protégé, Davis Love III, by 1 stroke. It had been 11 years since Crenshaw had won his first Masters and he was, at 43, the oldest Masters champion since Jack Nicklaus won in 1986 at the age of 46.

In an emotional speech after his victory, Crenshaw said: 'I had a 15th club in my bag today and that was Harvey – Harvey Penick. It's like someone put their hand on my shoulder this week and guided me through.'

A newspaper headline the next day echoed Crenshaw's sentiments: 'Touched By An Angel', it read.

NORMAN'S DAY-FOUR DISASTER
When a talented young Australian made his US Masters debut in 1981 and finished a tantalizing fourth, few doubted that he would one day pull on the coveted green jacket.

The man in question, Greg Norman, went on to win two Majors – the 1986 and 1993 British Opens – and dominate world golf for nearly a decade, spending a total of six years as the game's top ranked player. But victory at Augusta continued to elude him, although he finished tied second in 1986 and 1987, and tied third in 1989 and 1995.

So when the 'Great White Shark', as he came to be known, returned to Augusta's lush fairways and manicured greens in 1996 for his 15th Masters, and proceeded to shoot a course record 63 on the first day, it seemed that the golfing gods may finally have smiled on the World Number One.

Greg Norman sinks to his knees in despair as victory slips away during the 1996 US Masters.

By the end of day three, Norman had built up a seemingly insurmountable lead of 6 shots over his nearest competitor, Briton Nick Faldo, shooting just four bogeys in the first 54 holes. No-one in the history of Major golf had ever blown a 6-shot lead, but Norman proceeded to rewrite that record as he self-destructed on day four in one of the worst collapses ever seen in Major championship golf.

They say the Masters isn't over till the back nine on Sunday – and that's where Norman shot a 4-over-par 40, giving him a 6-over-par final round of 78 which included five bogeys and two double bogeys. Faldo, who shot a superb 67 – the best round of the day – eventually won by a startling 5 shots to collect his third Masters title.

Afterwards, Norman's response was short and to the point.

'I played like shit,' he said.

YEAR OF THE TIGER

Tiger Woods is undoubtedly the biggest sensation ever to hit the game of golf. In his teens, Woods enjoyed unprecedented successes as an amateur golfer – he won the US Junior Amateur for three consecutive years, the only person ever to win it more than once; and he was the youngest ever winner of the US Amateur Championship, which he also won on three consecutive occasions.

In late 1996, at the age of 20, he turned professional and immediately signed, among others, a US$40 million deal with Nike and a US$20 million deal with Titleist. He won the Las Vegas Invitational, his first event as a professional, and became the fastest player to win US$1 million – in just nine events – beating the previous record of 28 events held by South African Ernie Els.

Woods won again in the first event of the 1997 season, the Mercedes Championship, but it was in April of that year that Tiger Woods truly became a household name: he won the US Masters at Augusta, his first Major as a professional. But he didn't just win the event – he rewrote the record books. At 21 he was the youngest winner of the Masters and his 72-hole score of 270 was also a new record, beating the 271 set by Jack Nicklaus in 1965 and American Raymond Floyd in 1976. His winning margin of 12 shots was the biggest in a Major this century.

Woods is an ethnic mix of one-quarter black, one-quarter Chinese, one-quarter Thai, one-eighth Caucasian and one-eighth native American Indian and, apart from his Caucasian lineage, he was the first of any of these ethnic groups to win the Masters. Tiger is talented, telegenic and a sponsor's dream. It has been estimated that since he turned professional on 26 August 1996, a cash injection of over US$650 million has breathed new life into the game of golf – bigger sponsorships, bigger television deals, bigger prize-money... the game will never be the same.

The new face of world golf – Tiger Woods after winning the US Masters.

RULES IN BRIEF

In the game of golf, there are basically two forms of play: one which is decided by holes won and lost (matchplay) and the other which is decided by the total number of strokes taken to complete the round (strokeplay).

The following is a summary of the Rules of Golf, simplified where possible.

ETIQUETTE

Etiquette covers both courtesy and priority on the course, as well as care of the course. Whilst the following points are not Rules as such, they are an important part of the game.

- Don't move, talk or stand close to a player making a stroke.
- Don't play until the group in front is out of the way.
- Always play without delay. Leave the putting green as soon as all players in your group have holed out.
- Invite faster groups to play through.
- Replace divots; smooth footprints in bunkers.
- Don't step on the line of another player's putt.
- Don't drop clubs on the putting green.
- Replace the flagstick carefully.

DEFINITIONS

The Definitions section of the Rules of Golf contains over 40 Definitions which form the foundation around which the Rules of play are written. A good knowledge of the defined terms will help in the correct application of the Rules. These include:

- Teeing Ground – the starting place for the hole, defined by two tee-markers.
- Through the Green – the whole area of the golf course except the teeing ground and putting green of the hole being played, and all hazards.
- Hazards – any bunker or water hazard.
- Putting Green – an area specially prepared for putting and containing a 4.25in (10.8cm) diameter hole.
- Out-of-bounds – ground on which play is prohibited i.e. not part of the course. A ball is out-of-bounds when all of it lies out-of-bounds.
- Loose Impediments – natural objects such as stones, leaves and twigs, provided they are not

fixed or growing, are not solidly embedded and are not sticking to the ball.
- Obstructions – any man-made object, except:
  (a) objects defining out-of-bounds;
  (b) any part of an immovable man-made object which is out-of-bounds; and
  (c) any construction declared by the Committee in the Local Rules to be an integral part of the course.
- Casual Water – any temporary accumulation of water on the course which is visible before or after the player takes his stance (dew and frost are not casual water).
- Ground-under-repair (GUR) – any portion of the course so marked by the Committee. Also includes material piled for removal and a hole made by a greenkeeper, even if not so marked.

THE RULES OF PLAY
General Points
- Before commencing your round:
  (a) Read the Local Rules on the scorecard.
  (b) Put an identification mark on your ball. Many golfers play the same brand of ball and if you can't identify your ball, it's lost.
  (c) Count your clubs. You are allowed a maximum of 14 clubs.
- During the round, don't ask for 'advice' from anyone except your partner or caddie.
- During a hole you may not play a practice stroke.

Teeing Off
- Tee off between and not in front of the tee-markers. You may tee off up to two club-lengths behind the front line of the tee-markers.

Teeing off Outside this Area
- In matchplay there is no penalty but your opponent may ask you to replay your stroke; in strokeplay you incur a two-stroke penalty and must then play from within the proper area.

Playing the Ball
- Play the ball as it lies. Don't improve your lie, the area of your intended swing or your line of play by moving, bending or breaking anything fixed or growing except in fairly taking your stance or making your swing. Don't press anything down or build a stance.

- If your ball lies in a bunker or a water hazard, don't touch the ground in the bunker, or the ground or water in the water hazard, before your downswing.
- The ball must be fairly struck, not pushed or spooned.

Playing a Wrong ball (Except in a Hazard)
- In matchplay you lose the hole; in strokeplay you incur a two-stroke penalty and you must then play the correct ball.

On the Putting Green
- You may repair ball marks and old hole plugs on the line of your putt but not any other damage, including spike marks.
- You may mark, lift and clean your ball on the putting green. Always replace it on the exact spot.
- Don't test the putting surface by scraping it or rolling a ball over it.

Ball Played from Putting Green Strikes Flagstick
- In matchplay you lose the hole; in strokeplay you incur a two-stroke penalty.

Ball at Rest Moved
- If your ball is at rest and it is moved by you, your partner or your caddie except as permitted by the Rules or if it moves after you have addressed it, add a penalty stroke and replace your ball.
- If your ball is at rest and is moved by someone else or another ball, you may replace it without penalty to you.

Ball in Motion Deflected or Stopped
- If the ball struck by you is deflected or stopped by you, your partner or your caddie:
  (a) in matchplay you lose the hole;
  (b) in strokeplay you incur a two-stroke penalty and the ball is played as it lies.
- If the ball struck by you is deflected or stopped by someone else: Play your ball as it lies without penalty, except
(a) in matchplay, if an opponent or his caddie deflects the ball, you have an option to replay the stroke;
(b) in strokeplay, if the ball is deflected after a stroke from on the putting green, replay.

- If the ball struck by you is deflected or stopped by another ball at rest, no penalty is incurred and the ball is played as it lies, except
  - (a) in strokeplay you incur a two-stroke penalty if your ball and the other ball were on the putting green before you played.

Lifting, Dropping and Placing the Ball

- If a ball to be lifted is to be replaced, its position must be marked.
- If a ball is to be dropped or placed in any other position (e.g. taking relief from GUR, etc.), it is recommended that the ball's original position be marked.
- When dropping, stand erect, hold the ball at shoulder height and arm's length, and drop it. If a dropped ball strikes you or your partner, caddie or equipment, it must be re-dropped without penalty.
- There are eight instances where a dropped ball rolls to such a position that it must be re-dropped – see Rule 20-2c.

Ball Interfering with or Assisting Play

- You may lift your ball if it might assist any other player.
- You may have any ball lifted if it might interfere with your play or assist any other player.

Loose Impediments

- You may move a loose impediment unless it and your ball are in a hazard.
- If you have touched a loose impediment within one club-length of your ball and your ball moves, the ball must be replaced, and (unless your ball was on the putting green) you incur a penalty stroke.

Obstructions

- Check the Local Rules on the scorecard for guidance on immovable obstructions (e.g. surfaced roads and paths, etc).
- Movable obstructions (e.g. rakes, tin cans, etc.) anywhere on the course may be moved. If the ball moves it must be replaced without penalty.
- If an immovable obstruction (e.g. a water fountain) interferes with your stance or swing, you may drop the ball within one club-length of the nearest point of relief but not nearer to the hole. There is no relief for intervention on your line of play unless your ball and the obstruction are on the putting green.

Casual Water, Ground-under-repair, etc.

- If your ball is in casual water, ground-under-repair or a hole or cast made by a burrowing animal (e.g. a rabbit), you may drop without penalty within one club-length of the nearest point of relief but not nearer to the hole.

Water Hazards

- Check the Local Rules on the scorecard to establish whether the sea, lake, river, etc. is a 'water hazard' or a 'lateral water hazard'.

Ball in Water Hazard

- Play the ball as it lies or, under penalty of one stroke:
  - (a) drop any distance behind the water hazard, keeping a straight line between the hole, the point where the ball crossed the margin of the water hazard and the spot on which the ball is dropped, or
  - (b) play again from where you hit the ball into the hazard.

Ball in Lateral Water Hazard

- In addition to the options for a ball in a water hazard (see above), under penalty of one stroke, you may drop within two club-lengths of:
  - (a) the point where the ball crossed the margin of the hazard, or
  - (b) a point on the opposite side of the hazard equidistant from the hole.

Ball Lost or Out-of-bounds

- Check the Local Rules on the scorecard to identify the boundaries of the course.
- If your ball is lost outside a water hazard or out-of-bounds, you must play another ball from the spot where the last shot was played, under penalty of one stroke i.e. stroke and distance. You are allowed 5 minutes to search for a ball, after which if it is not found or identified, it is lost.
- If, after playing a shot, you think your ball may be lost outside a water hazard or out-of-bounds, you

may play a 'provisional ball'. You must state that it is a provisional ball and play it before you go forward to search for the original ball. If the original ball is lost or out-of-bounds, you must continue with the provisional ball under penalty of one stroke.

- If the original ball is not lost or out-of-bounds, you must continue play of the hole with it and the provisional ball must be abandoned.

Ball Unplayable

- If you believe your ball is unplayable outside a water hazard (and you are the sole judge), you may under penalty of one stroke:
- (a) drop within two club-lengths of where the ball lies, but not nearer the hole;
- (b) drop any distance behind the point where the ball lay, keeping a straight line between the hole, the point where the ball lay and the spot on which the ball is dropped, or
- (c) replay the shot.
- If your ball is in a bunker you may proceed under (a), (b) or (c). However, if you elect to proceed under (a) or (b), you must drop in the bunker.

A WORD OF ADVICE

A good score may be spoiled, or a match lost, due to a penalty incurred through ignorance or confusion concerning the Rules. A sound knowledge of the above summary should aid the golfer in tackling a 'Rule problem'. Nevertheless, the Complete Rules of Golf as approved by the Royal and Ancient Golf Club of St Andrews and the United States Golf Association should be consulted where any doubt may arise.

Copies of Golf Rules in Brief or the Complete Rules of Golf can be obtained from your club secretary; alternatively, send a stamped addressed envelope to:

Royal & Sunalliance Insurance,
Freepost (LV7075),
PO Box 144,
Liverpool L69 4HQ
United Kingdom

Queries concerning the Rules should be made through recognized Golf Clubs or Affiliated Unions of the R&A.

REGULATIONS RELATING TO GOLF CLUBS

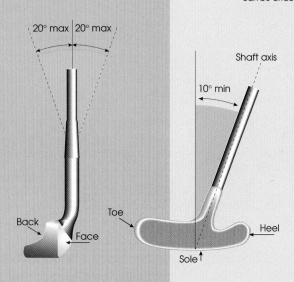

Non-regulation clubs

A golf club is defined as an implement designed to be used for striking the ball, while a putter is defined as a club with a loft of not more than 10 degrees, designed primarily for use on the putting green. Rule 4 of the Rules of Golf deals with golf clubs. Manufacturers are required to submit samples of new clubs to the Royal and Ancient Golf Club of St Andrews (or to the United States Golf Association) for a ruling on whether the clubs conform to Rule 4. A player's clubs must conform to the following regulations or he or she risks penalties or disqualification:

Design of the clubs

1. Club

The club must be composed of a shaft and a head and may not be significantly different from the traditional and customary form and make. Clubs other than putters may not be adjustable, other than for weight.

2. Shaft

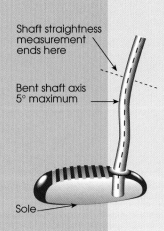

Shaft straightness measurement ends here

Bent shaft axis 5° maximum

Sole

- The shaft must be straight and have the same bending and twisting properties in any direction.
- It must be attached to the club head at the heel, directly or through a single neck or socket. The distance from the top of the neck to the sole of the club, measured along the axis and following any bends in the neck, must not exceed 5in (127mm). A putter shaft can be attached to any point on the head.
  - The shaft must be straight from the top of the grip to a point that measures no more than 5in (127mm) above the sole.
  - The length of the club must not be less than 18in (46cm) from the top of the grip to the sole of the club.
  - When the shaft is in its normal address position, the projection of the straight part of the shaft onto a vertical plane through the toe and heel must diverge from

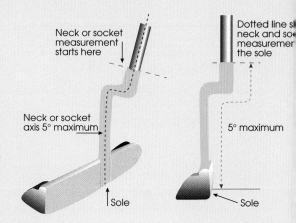

Neck or socket measurement starts here

Dotted line s[hows] neck and so[cket] measuremen[t] the sole

Neck or socket axis 5° maximum

Sole

5° maximum

Sole

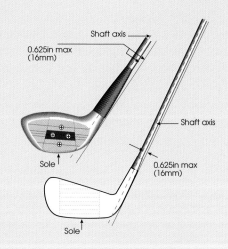

Shaft axis

0.625in max (16mm)

Shaft axis

Sole

0.625in max (16mm)

Sole

the vertical by at least 10 degrees. In addition, the projection of the straight part of the shaft onto the vertical plane along the line of play must not diverge from the vertical by more than 20 degrees.

- In all clubs except for putters, the heel of the club must lie within 0.625in (16mm) from a line parallel to the shaft axis.

20° max | 20° max

Shaft axis

10° min

Back

Toe

Face

Heel

Sole

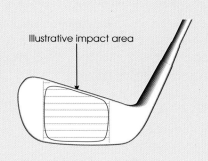

Illustrative impact area

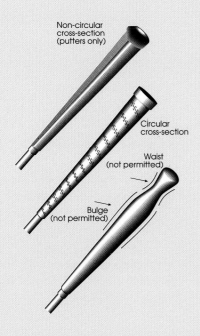

Non-circular
cross-section
(putters only)

Circular
cross-section

Waist
(not permitted)

Bulge
(not permitted)

- Holes through the head, transparent material (other than for decorative or structural purposes), appendages such as knobs, plates, rods or fins.
- The distance from the heel to the toe must be bigger than the distance from the face to the back of the club head.
- The club head may only have one striking face (except for putters which may have two faces provided their characteristics are the same and they are opposite each other).

5. Club Face

- The club face must be hard and rigid (although exceptions are made for putters). The impact area must be of a single material (although exceptions are made for wooden clubs).
- Markings in the impact area may not have sharp edges or raised lips. However, grooves or punch marks are permitted. The grooves must be straight with diverging sides and a symmetrical cross-section. The width and cross-section must be

3. Grip

- The grip must be straight and extend to the end of the shaft.
- For clubs other than putters, the grip must be circular in cross-section. Putter grips may be noncircular provided the cross-section is not concave in any part and is symmetrical and similar throughout the length of the grip.
- The grip can be tapered but cannot have a bulge or waist, or be moulded for the hands. The cross-section diameter must not exceed 1.75in (45mm).

Axis of Symmetry

Groove depth
max 0.02in
(0.5mm)

30°   30°

Examples of permissible groove cross-sections

4. Club Head

- The club head must be 'plain in shape'. Although it is not comprehensively defined, some features not allowed are:

Face → ← Back

A

Toe

Heel

0.625in
(16mm)

consistent across the face of the club and the length of the grooves. These specifications do not apply to putters.
- Foreign material may not be applied to the club face for the purpose of influencing the movement of the ball.

Number of Clubs

A player may not start a round of golf with more than 14 clubs in his bag. If a player starts a round with less than 14 clubs, he can add·extra clubs during the round provided the total does not exceed 14. A player can also replace, with any club, a club that becomes unfit for play during the normal course of play. Partners can share clubs so long as the total number of clubs carried by the partners is not more than 14.

GLOSSARY

Ace A hole-in-one.

Address The position a golfer assumes when he is preparing to hit the ball.

Albatross A score of three under par on a hole; also known as a double eagle.

Approach Usually a short- to medium-length shot played towards the putting green or pin, hence 'approach shot'.

Attend the flag To hold and then remove the flag while another player putts, a normal part of golfing etiquette during a round.

Back nine The last nine holes of an 18-hole golf course.

Backspin The spin on a ball caused by the club face; stops the ball rolling forward when it lands.

Backswing The first part of the golf swing when the club is taken away from the ball.

Bail out Hitting to avoid trouble, e.g. well left to avoid a hazard on the right.

Balata Sap from a tropical tree, used to make covers for golf balls.

Ball-marker A small round object used to mark the position of the ball on the green when it is picked up.

Ball-washer A device used to clean your golf ball.

Best ball (also called betterball) The best score on a hole by two or more partners in a best-ball match.

Birdie A score of one under par on a hole.

Blind shot A shot played when you can't see the spot where you want the ball to land.

Block A shot that flies straight but to the right of the target.

Bogey A score of one over par on a hole.

Break (also borrow) The curve of the ball when putted due to the slope of the green.

Bunker A sand trap on a golf course, defined as a hazard.

Buried ball/lie When part of the ball is below the surface of the sand in a bunker.

Caddie A person who carries a golfer's clubs and who may give golfer advice on course strategy and club selection.

Carry The distance a golf ball must travel from where it is hit to where it lands on the ground (used particularly when judging the distance over a hazard).

Casual water A temporary accumulation of water on a golf course, from which you are entitled to relief.

Centre-shafted A putter in which the shaft is joined to the centre of the head.

Chip A short, lofted shot played from close to the green.

Chip-in A chip that finds the hole.

Choke down To hold the club lower on the grip.

Cleat The spike on the sole of a golf shoe.

Closed club face The club is angled towards the feet; one's stance is closed if the front foot is across the target line.

Club-length The distance from the end of the grip to the head.

Compression The degree of resilience of a golf ball.

Concede To give an opponent a putt, hole or match.

Course rating A comparison of various golf courses in terms of difficulty, using various criteria.

Crosswind A wind blowing from right to left or vice versa.

Cut A score that eliminates a percentage of the field.

Cut shot A shot that curves from left to right.

Divot A piece of turf removed by a golf club in the process of playing a shot.

Dog-leg A left or right bend in the fairway of a golf hole.

Dormie When a competitor leads by as many holes as there are left to play in matchplay.

Double-bogey A score of two over par on a hole.

Downhill lie When the right foot is higher than the left at address (for right-handers).

Downswing The part of the golf swing from the top of the backswing through to impact with the ball.

Draw A shot that produces a controlled right-to-left movement of the ball.

Drive A shot from a tee other than on par-three holes.

Drive the green When your drive finishes on the putting surface.

Driver A 1-wood, used for getting the most distance off the tee.

Driving range An area set aside for practising shots.

Drop A player drops his ball from shoulder height when he has an unplayable lie or when his ball is lost.

Duck hook A shot that curves severely from right to left.

Eagle A score of two under par on a hole.

Etiquette A golfing code of conduct.

Executive course A shorter than normal golf course featuring mainly par three and par four holes.

Extra holes Played when a match finishes even.

Face The part of the club head that strikes the ball.

Fade A shot that produces a controlled left-to-right movement of the ball.

Fairway The area between the tee and the green with short, trimmed grass.

Fairway woods 2, 3, 4, 5 and also higher numbered woods, designed to be used off the fairway or when the ball is in play off the tee.

Fat shot To hit the ground before the ball.

First cut The strip of rough at the edge of the fairway.

Flat swing A low club path around the body.

Flex The amount of bend in a shaft.

Flier A shot that travels much too far, usually played from the rough.

Follow-through The part of the golf swing after impact with the ball.

Fore! A warning shouted by a golfer when a ball may be in danger of hitting another player.

Forged irons Clubs made one by one, without a mould.

Fourball Four golfers playing together, usually two a side, each with their own ball; the better score of each team at each hole counts.

Foursome Four golfers playing together, or a match in which two pairs play against each other, each side using only one ball.

Free drop A drop where no penalty is incurred.

Fringe The area of slightly longer grass around the green.

Front nine The first nine holes of an 18-hole golf course.

Gallery The spectators at a tournament.

Grain The direction in which the blades of grass point on a green.

Green The area of a golf hole designed for putting, with short, well-manicured grass.

Green fee The price charged to play a round of golf on a course.

Greens in regulation The number of greens reached in the regulation number of shots.

Greenside Close to the green.

Grip The top part of a golf club held by the golfer; also the manner in which a club is held.

Gross score Your score before you make your handicap deduction.

Ground-under-repair An area on the golf course that is undergoing maintenance or repair.

Hacker A bad player.

Half When opponents make the same score; a match is halved if it ends 'all square'.

Handicap A system designed to allow golfers of all levels to compete with each other; it is an allowance in strokes based on previous performances.

Hanging lie A ball that is on the ground sloping downwards, ahead of a golfer.

Hardpan Very firm turf.

Hazard Any obstructive or difficult feature on a golf course, e.g. lakes, bunkers.

High-handicapper A mediocre player.

Hole-in-one Hitting the ball into the hole with only one stroke.

Hole out To finish play on a hole.

Honour The privilege of teeing off first, usually given to the player who recorded the lowest score on the previous hole.

Hook A shot where the ball curves away sharply from right to left.

Hosel The hollow part of a club head which is attached to the shaft.

In play Within the boundaries of the golf course.

Inside The area on the player's side of a line drawn from the ball to the target.

Kick Another word for bounce.

Ladies' day A day on which the course is reserved for lady golfers only.

Laid off When the club points to the left of the target at the top of the backswing.

Lateral water hazard A ditch, stream or lake roughly parallel to the line of the hole.

Lay up Play a shot conservatively to avoid trouble.

Leaderboard Board on which the lowest scores are posted.

Lie The position in which a ball lands on the golf course; also the angle between the club head and the shaft.

Links A golf course situated next to the ocean, typically on barren, treeless terrain.

Lip-out When the ball touches the edge of the hole but doesn't drop.

Local Rules Those dealing with unusual features of a particular golf course.

Loft The angle on the club head which gives more or less height to the ball when it is struck.

Long game Shots in which achieving distance is important.

Loose impediments Any natural objects that are not growing, solidly embedded or stuck to the ball.

Low-handicapper A good player.

Make To hole a shot.

Makeable A shot with a good chance of being holed.

Mark Identifying the spot on the green where a player has picked up his ball.

Marker The player who keeps another player's score.

Matchplay A competition based on number of holes won; the winning player wins more holes than are left to play.

Medal play (also called strokeplay) A competition based on the number of strokes played. The player with the lowest number of strokes wins.

Metal wood A wood made of metal.

Misclub To use the wrong club for a particular distance.

Miss the cut To be eliminated from an event because your score is too high.

Mixed foursome A team consisting of two men and two women.

Mulligan The opportunity to replay your last shot.

Nassau A bet in which a round of 18 holes is divided into three – front nine, back nine and full 18.

Nett score Your score after making a handicap deduction.

Niblick An old Scottish term for a 9-iron.

Nineteenth hole The clubhouse bar.

Obstructions Any man-made objects, except objects that define out-of-bounds, or are part of an immovable man-made object that is out-of-bounds, or a construction that is ruled to be a part of the course.

Off-centre hit A strike that is not solid.

Offset A club with the head set behind the shaft.

One-putt To take only one putt to sink the ball on a green.

One-up One hole ahead in the match score.

Open club head When club head is turned out at the toe; an open stance is when the line of the feet is to the left of the target (for a right-handed player).

Out-of-bounds The area outside the defined area of a golf course, generally marked by a line of posts or fences.

Outside Area on the far side of a line drawn from the ball to the target.

Overclub To use a club that hits the ball too far.

Par The standard score in strokes assigned to each hole on a golf course, given on the scorecard.

Parkland course Typically an inland golf course laid out on rich grassland with little rough.

Penal Difficult.

Penalty stroke An additional stroke or strokes added to a golfer's score for an infringement of the rules.

PGA Professional Golfers Association.

Pin The flagstick, which marks the location of the hole.

Pin high A ball that is on the green and even with the pin but off to one side.

Pin placement The location of the hole on the green.

Pitch shot Generally an approach shot to the green, but longer than a chip.

Pitch mark An indentation on the green made by the ball when it lands.

Play-off Where two or more players tie and play extra holes to determine a winner.

Playing through When a slower group invites the group behind them to pass.

Plugged lie When the ball finishes half buried in the turf.

Plumb-bob To line up a putt with one eye closed and with the putter held vertically in front of the face.

Pot bunker A small, steep-sided bunker.

Practice green Most golf clubs have a green with many holes for practising putting.

Preferred lies Temporary rule allowing the ball to be moved to a better position because of wet conditions.

Pro-am A competition in which professionals team up with amateurs.

Public course A golf course open to anyone.

Provisional ball If a golfer suspects that his ball may be lost, he plays a provisional ball as a time-saving measure. The provisional ball becomes the ball in play if the original ball is indeed lost.

Pull A shot that flies straight to the left of the target.

Punch A shot hit lower with the ball back in the stance.

Push A shot that flies straight to the right of the target.

Putt A rolling shot played on the green.

Putter The club designed for putting.

Qualifying school An event where aspiring golfers try to qualify for the professional tours.

Reading the green Judging the path on which a putt must travel to the hole.

Recovery A shot played into a good position from a bad lie or unfavourable position.

Regular A club shaft with normal flex.

Release The point in the downswing where the wrists uncock.

Relief When a golfer is allowed to lift the ball and then drop it in another area under the Rules of Golf.

Rifle a shot To hit the ball hard, straight and far.

Rough The area of the golf course alongside the fairways where the grass is thicker and longer.

Rub of the green When a ball is stopped or deflected by an outside agency; there is no penalty and the ball is played as it lies.

Run The roll of the ball after landing.

Sand wedge The most lofted iron, for playing out of bunkers or for playing pitches.

Scorecard A card on which to record your score; this card also reflects hole length, par and hole rating.

Set of clubs The maximum allowed is 14, usually four woods, nine irons and a putter.

Scratch A handicap of zero; a person who plays to par.

Second cut The second level of rough, higher than the first cut and further from the fairway.

Set-up *See* Address.

Shank A shot struck by the club's hosel that travels directly to the right (for a right-handed player).

Shooting the lights out To play very well.

Short game Describes approach shots to the green and putting.

Sidehill lie When the ball lies above or below your feet.

Sink To hole a putt.

Skins A betting game where the lowest score on a hole wins the pot; if the hole is tied, the money carries over to the next hole.

Slice A shot that curves sharply from left to right.

Sky A ball that flies off the top of the club face and travels very high and short.

Sleeve of balls A box of three golf balls.

Snap hook A severe hook. *See* also Duck hook.

Spot putting Aiming for a point on the green over which the ball must go if it is to eventually find the hole.

Square When addressing the ball and the body is parallel to the line of the ball to the target.

Stableford A type of competition against par using seven-eighths of handicap according to the stroke index; nett par scores 2 points, one over 1 point and birdie 3 points.

Stance The position a golfer assumes when he is preparing to play the ball.

Starter The person running the order of play from the first tee.

Starting time Your tee-off time from the first tee.

Stiff When club shaft has reduced flex.

Stroke A movement of the club to hit the ball.

Stroke and distance A penalty of one stroke plus returning to the spot from where the ball was played when a ball is lost, unplayable, or out-of-bounds.

Stroke index The difficulty rating of holes on a golf course, whereby strokes are allocated according to a golfer's handicap.

Strokeplay A competition decided by the number of shots played.

Sudden-death A form of play-off where the first player to win a hole wins the match.

Swale A dip or depression on the golf course.

Sweet spot The perfect place on the club face to strike the ball.

Swing weight A measure of the balance and overall weight of golf clubs.

Takeaway The early part of the backswing.

Tee A peg on which the ball is placed for driving; also, the area from which the ball is hit.

Tee up To start play.

Thin (also skull) To hit the ball above its equator.

Three off the tee If a golfer's tee shot is lost, unplayable or out-of-bounds, he is penalized one stroke and must play off the tee again.

Three-putt To take three putts on the green to hole the ball.

Threesome Three golfers playing together (each using his/her own ball); or two golfers using the same ball and playing alternate strokes against a single golfer.

Throughswing The part of the golf swing during which the ball is actually hit.

Through the green The whole of the golf course except hazards, and the teeing area and putting green of the hole being played.

Top Hitting the ball above its centre, causing it to roll or hop along the ground.

Trajectory The flight of the ball.

Triple bogey A score of three over par on a hole.

'The turn' The halfway mark on an 18-hole golf course.

Two-putt To take two putts on the green to sink the ball.

Underclub To use at least one club less than you should for a particular distance.

Unplayable A player may deem a ball unplayable and, taking a penalty stroke, may drop the ball but no nearer the hole.

Up Ahead in a match; or the next person to play.

Up and down To get the ball into the hole in two strokes from somewhere off the green.

Uphill lie When the ball lies on ground sloping upwards in front of a player.

Upright A steep swing.

Water hazard A pond, lake or stream.

Wedge A lofted club used for pitching.

Wrist cock The natural hinging of the wrists on the backswing.

Yips An uncontrollable twitching, caused by nerves, which affects golfers when putting or chipping.

INDEX

Page numbers in bold denote photographs.

PHOTOGRAPHIC CREDITS

The following all Touchline Photo/Allsport (individual photographers in alphabetical order): pp16 (right), 17 (2nd from right), 18 (centre), 23 (far right), 40 (top), 43 (top), 45 (top), 48–49, 58 (bottom), 116 (bottom), 132 (top), 134–35 (top row, left), 142 (right), 144 (top), 151; **Tom Able Green** p 160; **David Allen** p13 (top); **Howard Boylan** p115; **Simon Bruty** p19 (top row, centre), 145 (right); **David Cannon** cover (main photo & front flap), endpapers, title page (left), pp16 (left), 17 (3rd from left), 18 (right), 19 (top row, left & right; middle row, right; bottom row), 23 (centrepage), 24–25, 27 (top right), 28 (right), 30, 32–33, 36, 38–39, 41 (bottom), 42 (left top & bottom), 45 (bottom), 56–57, 73, 91, 92–93, 111 (left bottom), 112 (bottom right), 117 (top row, left; middle row, centre & right; bottom row, right), 126 (top & bottom), 130 (top), 131 (top & bottom), 132 (bottom), 134–35 (top row, 2nd from right & right; middle row, second from left; bottom row, second from right), 144 (bottom), 145 (left), 146, 147 (right), 152; **Graham Chadwick** pp 114, 148; **Chris Cole** p31 (bottom); **J D Cuban** pp19 (middle row, left), 35 (right), 61 (right bottom); **Stephen Dunn** pp119, 134–35 (bottom row, left); **Jon Ferrey** pp66–67, 141 (right); **Scott Halleran** p59 (bottom right); **Hobbs Collection** pp 17 (far right), 18 (left); **Michael Hobbs** p16 (centre), 17 (far left); **Phil Inglis** p42 (right), 89, 1 (top left); **Rusty Jarrett** p51 (bottom centre); **Craig Jones** p37 (right), 40 (bottom), 41 (top right), 59 (top left), 64–65, 111 (top right), 117 top row, righ 134–35 (middle row, left); **Alex Livesey** p139 (top right); **Andy Lyons** p12–13, 60 (bottom left), 112 (bottom left), 134–35 (middle row, second from right Clive Mason** p117 (middle row, left); **Tim Matthews** p23 (top row, 2nd from right); **Don Morley** p142 (top left); **Stephen Munday** foreword (left), pp3 (left), 43 (bottom right), 58 (top), 60 (top left), 113, 116 (top left), 117 (bottom row, left), 127 (top), 138 (bottom left), 147 (left); **Gary Newkirk** cover spin p26–27, 50 (cavity back); **Andrew Redington** foreword (right), p43 (bottom left), 74–75, 116 (top right), 133 (bottom); **David Rogers** p28 (left), 128–2 **Paul Severn** p22 (top & bottom), 34–35, 41 (top left), 106–107, 120–121, 127 (bottom), 133 (top); **Jamie Squire** imprint page, p23 bottom right, 52 (right) 134–35 (bottom row, right); **Matthew Stockman** p17 (2nd from left); **Anton Want** p130 (bottom).

ADDITIONAL PHOTOGRAPHERS: *Compleat Golfer* Photo Library pp 13 (bottom), 14–15, 48 (golf balls), 54 (bottom), 138 (top & bottom right), 139 (top left); **Gary Player Group** pp23 (top row, far left, 2nd from left & centre), 76–88, 95–105, 136 (top & bottom), 137 (bottom); **International Press Agency (INPRA)** pp 20–21, 134–35 (top row, second from left; middle row, far right; bottom row, 2nd from left), 136–37, 139 (centre), 140, 141 (left), 143; **Photo Access** pp108–09, **Photo Access/Peter Gridley** contents page; **Alain Proust** pp10–11, 122–23, 124 (top & bottom), 125; **Struik Image Library** p108 (etch); **Struik Image Library/Kelly Walsh** cover (deep etches & back flap), half title, full title (right), pp26 (top), 31 (right top, centre & bottom), 34 (top), 46–47, 48 (top), 49 (far right), 50 (except cavity back), 51 (left & far right), 52 (left), 53, 54 (deep etches), 55, 59 (golf bags), 60 (bottom right), 60–61, 61 (top right), 62 (top left & bottom right), 63, 66 (top); **Hetty Zantman** pp62 (bottom left & top right), 70, 71, 72, 110, 111 (centre), 112 (top right).